Wright to Gehry

Drawings from the collection of Barbara Pine

NEIL BINGHAM

Curated by Margaret Richardson

The Soane Gallery 2005

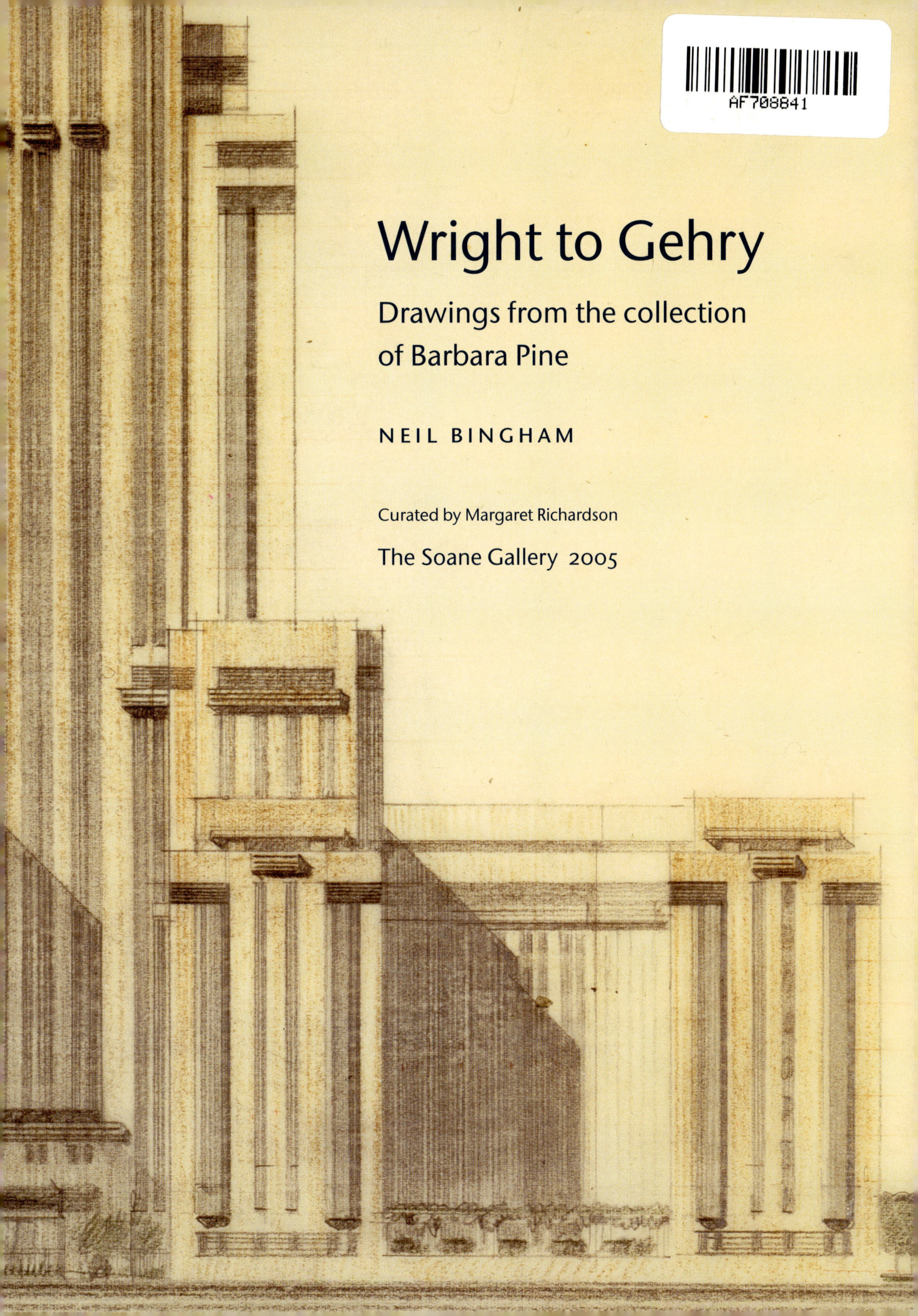

Wright to Gehry: Drawings from the Collection of Barbara Pine
An exhibition at Sir John Soane's Museum
21 April – 27 August 2005

Published in Great Britain 2005
by Sir John Soane's Museum

Reg. Charity No. 313609
www.soane.org

ISBN 0 9549041 1 7

The Trustees of Sir John Soane's Museum would like to thank the benefactors, patrons and sponsors whose annual donations support the Museum's exhibition and education programmes.

PATRONS

Pam and Philip Baldwin David and Molly Borthwick Debby and James Brice Richard Broyd Arnold Burton Peter and Marya Egerton Warburton Christopher Forbes Claire and Richard Gapper Richard and Sheila Griffiths Peter Hall Charles and Kaaren Hale Frances and David Hickman Michael and Beatrice Hoare John and Rowena Jackson Danny and Gry Katz Crispin Kelly James Kessler Laurence and Janet Kinney Victoria Legge-Bourke Oscar and Margaret Lewisohn Lulu and Charlie Lytle Christopher and Henrietta McCall Sir Richard MacCormac Katherine McCormick Mallet Rick Mather Richard and Rosemary Millar Michael and Jan Moore John W Murray William Parker Lord and Lady Phillimore Robin and Ann Purchas Lisbet Rausing and Peter Baldwin Leopold de Rothschild Alex and Elinor Sainsbury Nicholas and Elodie Stanley Alan and Ciannait Tait Chloe Teacher Andrew Templeton Michael Turner Simon Weil Jane and Michael Wilson

RECENT EXHIBITION SPONSORS

The Henry Moore Foundation *Thomas Banks 1735–1850: Britain's First Modern Sculptor*
Lisbet Rausing and Peter Baldwin *Raymond Erith 1904–1973: Progressive Classicist*
J Paul Getty Charitable Trust *Saving Wotton: The Remarkable Story of a Soane Country House*
The Designation Challenge Fund *Hooked on Books: The Library of Sir John Soane, Architect 1753–1837*
The Heritage Lottery Fund *William West and the Regency Toy Theatre*
Howard de Walden Estates Limited *'Bob the Roman': Heroic Antiquity and the Architecture of Robert Adam*

For information on exhibition sponsorship and how to support the Museum as an individual Patron or through a company, trust or foundation please contact the development office at Sir John Soane's Museum, 13 Lincoln's Inn Fields, London WC2A 3BP
Tel: 020 7440 4241

Designed and typeset in ITC Stone Sans by Libanus Press, Marlborough
Printed by BAS Printers, Salisbury

Front cover: William Lescaze, Design for the Garret A. Hobart III house and studio, 1938 (detail) (cat. 31)
Back cover: Steven Holl, Design for housing, 1986 (detail) (cat. 55)
Title page: Paul Philippe Cret, Design for a monumental building, *c.*1935 (detail) (cat. 30)
Page 9: Richard Meier, Design for an armchair, *c.*1979 (detail) (cat. 41)

Contents

Preface *Margaret Richardson* 5

Acknowledgements *Neil Bingham* 5

Introduction *Margaret Richardson* 7

THE CATALOGUE

The Barbara Pine Collection *Neil Bingham* 10

Catalogue entries *Neil Bingham* 13

Neil Bingham biography 48

SPONSORS OF THE EXHIBITION

The Conran Foundation
SOANE LTD
James and Shirley Sherwood

MEDIA PARTNER

BLUEPRINT

Preface

John Soane's personal expertise as a collector is best demonstrated by his collection of some 30,000 architectural drawings, which not only included designs by the great masters but also sketches and working drawings by his contemporaries Adam, Dance and Playfair, showing how interested he was in the whole process of design. So there could be no better place than the Soane to exhibit the private collection of Barbara Pine, another collector fascinated by the art of architectural drawing. My warmest thanks are due to her for allowing her drawings to cross the Atlantic for their first showing in London.

I am very grateful to Neil Bingham for his professionalism in researching and writing the Catalogue and to Stephen Astley, Will Palin, Susan Palmer and Margaret Schuelein who have helped in different ways to prepare the exhibition.

Our sponsors have made the exhibition happen so we are grateful to Blueprint, our media partner, to James and Shirley Sherwood, Lulu Lytle of SOANE LTD and especially to our principal sponsor Sir Terence Conran and the Conran Foundation.

MARGARET RICHARDSON
Curator, 2005

Acknowledgements

I am grateful to the following for their help on the Catalogue:

Artus Concepcion; Basile Baudez; Andre Bideau; Marino Fanti; Pascale Gibon; Dirk van den Heuvel; Nicholas Krasno; Liliane Liesens, Archives d'Architecture Moderne, Brussels; Eduardo Viehra; Dr Wolfgang Voight, Deutsches Architektur-Museum, Frankfurt-am-Main; Mariet Willinge, Nederlands Architectuurinstitut, Rotterdam; Karin Winter & Jonas Malmdal, Arkitekturmuseet – Swedish Museum of Architecture, Stockholm; William Wittaker, The Architectural Archives, University of Pennsylvania, Philadelphia

NEIL BINGHAM

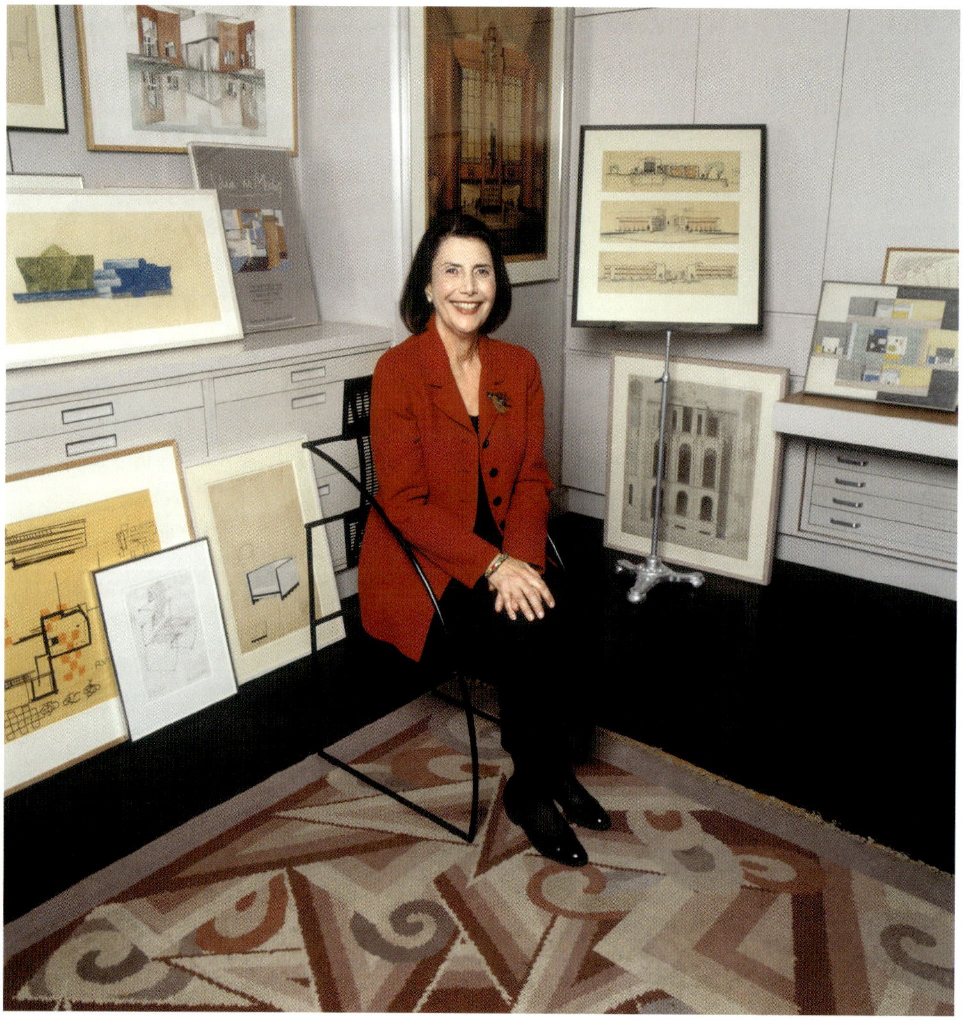

Barbara Pine in her study in New York, 2005 *Photograph: Robin Holland*

Introduction

MARGARET RICHARDSON

This exhibition consists of architectural drawings from the collection of Barbara Pine. It is one of the finest collections of contemporary architectural drawings in private hands and was begun in the 1970s just before drawings of this kind had become a commercial commodity.

But how did Barbara Pine begin collecting? She was born in Chicago – a precious city, as she says, to be brought up in if you like buildings, and was educated at Northwestern University where she studied Architectural History. Wright and Sullivan were especially important to her and her first acquisition was actually an architectural artefact, the metal elevator gate from Louis Sullivan's Chicago Stock Exchange which she purchased from an antique dealer. She was able to communicate this liking for architecture when she joined the Education Department at the Chicago Art Institute where she worked from 1959 to 1963.

Barbara Pine left Chicago in 1963 and settled in New York where she became involved with the world of design and architecture, becoming a member of the Junior Council at the Museum of Modern Art and devoting time and money to artists' books and video projects there. In the early 1970s there were the early stirrings of interest in Europe and America in contemporary architectural drawings as works of art in their own right rather than as functional documents – 'letters to the builder', as Lutyens often called them. In London the RIBA Heinz Gallery opened in 1972, pioneering an early series of exhibitions of architectural drawings, and in New York in the same year a penthouse show called 'Notations' at MoMA, organized by Martha Beck, (who later became Director of the Drawings Center), exhibited drawings of dance notations as well as architectural drawings by Hans Hollein.

Barbara Pine has often said that the idea for collecting architectural drawings came about when she first met Michael Graves. She had been to Princeton in the early 70s – before the 1972 Notations show – on a tour with the Architectural League and Graves was taking the group around to see his buildings there. Barbara was much attracted by his murals and began to think about what wonderful drawings he must do. She asked him about his drawings but he was not sure about selling them at the time. Later Barbara Pine was able to purchase Graves's designs for his own warehouse conversion in Princeton which she much admired, and which is in this exhibition (cat. 45). As Graves wrote in 1987 in the Foreword of the first exhibition of her Collection at Northwestern University, 'Years ago, on the hottest July day in the history of man (or so she thought), Barbara Pine came to my office in Princeton and patiently went through sketchbooks and drawings for a series of projects, hoping to find, as she eventually did, something that had meaning for her. This was the first time anyone had come to my office expressly to look at drawings with the intention of buying them for a collection.'

But Barbara Pine's first actual purchase in the early 1970s was the 1967 design by Richard Meier for his Hoffman House at East Hampton, New York (cat. 40). A friend, Henry Smith-Miller, suggested she should visit Meier: he wasn't, like so many architects at the time, throwing out drawings, and she found his work exciting and his drawings beautiful. Meier was also not averse to selling as he could see that there was beginning to be a market out there for drawings, separately from the owners of his buildings. She became a good friend as she did with Graves, Frank Gehry and many others and she kept up with new buildings and became very well informed about modern architecture. She visited many architectural offices and took time with people. Gehry, for example, was comparatively unknown in the early 1980s but Barbara was much attracted by his work at the time and particularly admired his lamp designs for the Formica Corporation and acquired the examples in the exhibition (cat. 52).

After the landmark exhibition, 'The Architecture of the École des Beaux-Arts' in 1975 at MoMA, museums and collectors came to realize how stylish and beautiful architectural drawings could be and at about this date both Sotheby's and Christie's in London began to hold sales of architectural drawings in their own right, rather than including them in general watercolour sales. Galleries specializing in architectural drawings – notably Max Protech who dealt in modern drawings – opened in New York – something which Barbara welcomed because as she said 'it makes it more enjoyable to know that the dealers have some drawings and to know I can go and talk about things'. It also expanded her collecting horizons as she could now collect examples of the work of great masters of the earlier 20th-century architects like Sant'Elia, Josef Hoffman, Eric Mendelsohn, Hans Poelzig, Le Corbusier and Gunnar Asplund, all of whom are represented in this exhibition.

Several things govern Barbara's choice of drawings. To begin with she has wide interests – in art and architecture (as well as in music), and in design – interior design – as well as the design of artefacts. She is particularly interested in furniture and owns several chairs designed by architects in her beautiful New York apartment, some relating to the designs she owns. Then she has a perceptive, well-informed eye and, as Neil Bingham demonstrates in his catalogue essay, there are often subconscious relationships between many of her acquisitions.

Barbara Pine's collection is small: she has some 160 drawings at present which are housed in her small study. She has very few large drawings and prefers to choose drawings which express condensed ideas on paper to fit her condensed spaces. In fact the particular strength of her collection lies in its high percentage of process or concept drawings in the architect's hand which reveal the progression of creative ideas at an early stage in a building's development. Because she buys only one or two drawings by each architect she tries to find a sheet which expresses, as she says, 'the essence of an architect's work'. She is unusual in liking this type of drawing as so often in this field it is the finished perspective or presentation elevations or sections which are highly valued and regularly exhibited and illustrated in books – in fact often the early sketches have not survived at all. Of course, Barbara Pine does also own many finished drawings often because they have become rare, surviving collectibles in their own right, but many of the later works by living architects are sketches in their own hands. As a member of the Architecture and Design and Drawings Committees at MoMA, Barbara Pine is in a good position to encourage the Museum to collect process drawings illustrating experimentation rather than the more visually attractive presentation perspectives – something which she is keen to do. Even in these days of computer-aided design, architects will continue to sketch out their early ideas and thoughts.

Above all, Barbara Pine is interested in architecture and this well-informed interest has guided her collecting. She knows architects and listens to their ideas; she puts herself into the mind of the architect. In buying she takes a straightforward approach and makes an offer. Often architects are her friends and she finds it rewarding to see how their careers have developed. She has participated in their adventure for the last thirty years and will continue to do so.

The Catalogue

NEIL BINGHAM

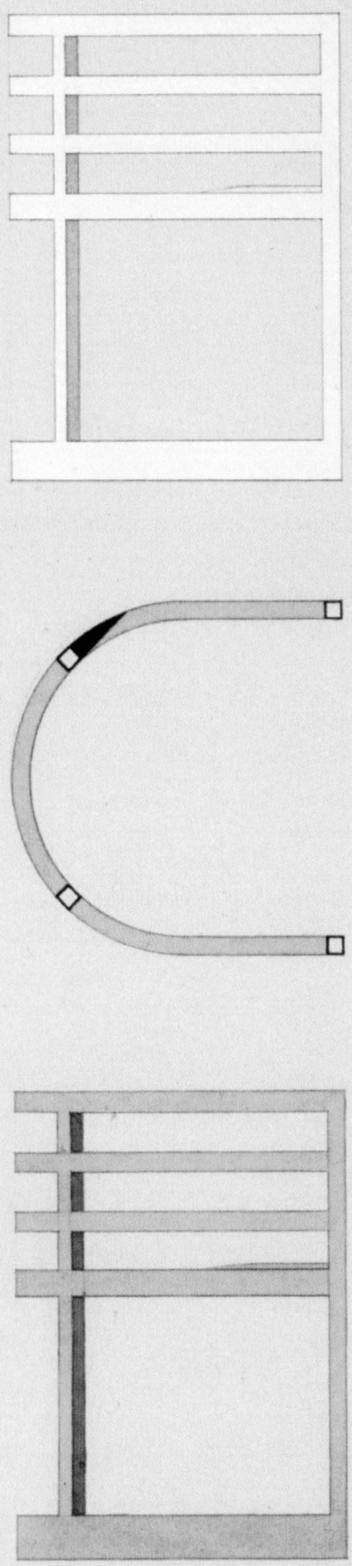

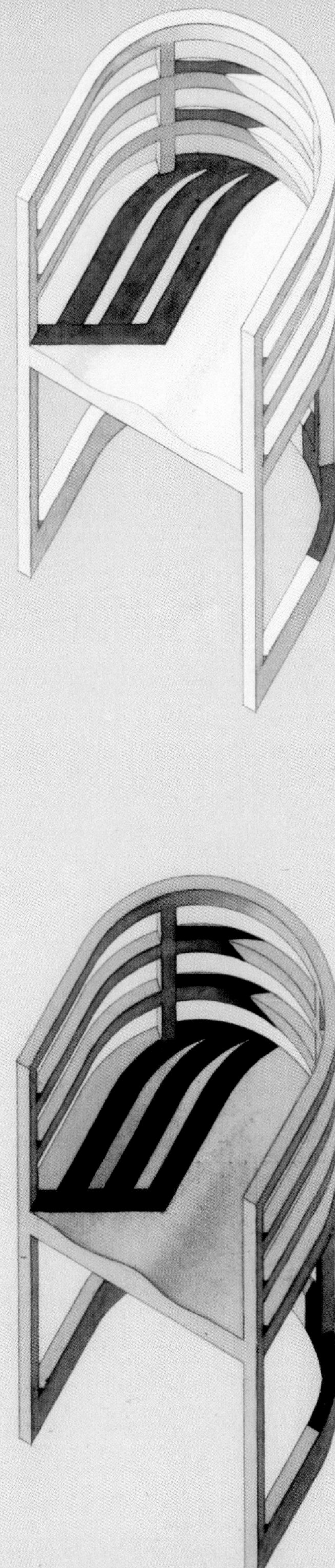

The Barbara Pine Collection

NEIL BINGHAM

Barbara Pine's collection of drawings acknowledges that architecture and object-based design are interdependent and of equal significance. This is a modern concept. Traditional collecting assigned architecture to the top of the artistic tree alongside, for example, painting and sculpture, assuming that furniture, interiors, household and industrial objects played a secondary role in the creative process. However, major modern collections, such as that of the Museum of Modern Art, New York (MoMA) – a collection which Barbara Pine knows intimately through her honorary position as a member of both the Architecture and Design and Drawings Committees – have broken down barriers of supremacies within design.

A consequence of this blurring of boundaries is that drawings of the design process themselves have now reached a point of interest as relevant as the very building or object they represent. Whereas once the design drawing was considered but a progressive stage to the final product, as ephemeral as the paper it was drawn upon, today's museums and galleries, and important collectors such as Barbara Pine, acquire drawings understanding that the drawing is as aesthetically and intellectually intriguing as the finished product.

In her Upper East Side apartment, Barbara Pine emphasises this correlation by placing design drawings alongside related objects: a framed finished drawing by Richard Meier of one of his armchairs (cat. 41) hangs near the actual white lacquered armchair made by Knoll; a sketch highlighting the curving perforated steel seat and back of the Quinta chair by Mario Botta (cat. 54) is displayed next to one of the actual chairs – Barbara Pine has more than half a dozen Botta chair designs in her collection; a pencil exercise in cardboard construction from Frank Gehry's Easy Edge series of furniture (cat. 51) overlooks the strange form of a real cardboard rocker which was made for the same series. And although these pieces stand on a large Art Deco carpet by Marion Dorn, the British textile designer from whom Barbara Pine may have no drawings, she does possess two extremely important designs by Eileen Gray, dating from about 1925, of the *Centimetré* and *Marine d'Abord* rugs for Gray's own seaside villa (cats 17 and 18).

Barbara Pine has a collection of over 160 drawings (and growing), and more than a third of these focus upon furniture and room interior designs, about the same ratio in the 60 drawings shown in this exhibition. Of these, the majority are for chairs, indicative not only of Barbara Pine's particular interest, but more broadly of the fascination that the chair has held for architects and designers in the twentieth century.

The earliest furniture drawings in the collection form an interesting group which illustrate the associations within stylistic movements and the relationships between designers found throughout this collection. This early set dates from the first years of the twentieth century. The spiritual leader of the period is here, Charles Rennie Mackintosh, with a design for an oak armchair (cat. 4). Mackintosh had a profound influence upon the Viennese school of Arts and Crafts, the Wiener Werkstätte and its two founders Koloman Moser and Josef Hoffmann, both of whom are represented: Moser by an *armoire* complete with the typical black and white check pattern (cat. 3), and Hoffmann with several designs including one for an interior with walls papered in one of his Wiener Werkstätte patterns (cat. 8). There is even, from a later period in Hoffmann's career, a design for a bent plywood chair (cat. 10). And then, rounding out this group is a design by George Mann Niedecken for a hall chair made in conjunction with America's most famous architect, Frank Lloyd Wright (cat. 5).

It is also possible to link other drawings to this group. Most obvious is the beautiful student design for a mausoleum by Franz Schwarz, who was a pupil of Hoffmann (cat. 6). Then there are two later designs by Frederick Kiesler from the 1940s, one of which is in this exhibition (cat. 35) – Kiesler was born and studied in Vienna under the influence of the Wiener Werkstätte, although in these furniture designs he is pursing his own restless quest for 'endlessness'. Finally, from as late as the 1970s, is the Richard Meier armchair, a modern interpretation of one of Hoffmann's finest bentwood armchairs (cat. 41).

Links of this type illustrate how the private collector's eye and mind work. Museums have detailed collecting policies to ensure their holdings remain cohesive and to fill gaps. Acquisitions are made cautiously, often after group deliberation, within set parameters. Although most collectors rarely can rival such comprehensiveness, they have the advantage of letting personal taste dictate purchases. This makes for associations within a collection that are highly individual to the collector.

As an example, having been born and raised in Chicago, Barbara Pine is naturally attracted to acquiring works from the Chicago School and other well-known architects from her windy city. She is intrigued by a working drawing she possesses from the practice of Adler & Sullivan, for the Chicago Auditorium Building, dating from about 1887, which shows a section through the theatre (cat. 1). Frank Lloyd Wright was working in the office at the time and she enjoys speculating that this matter-of-fact drawing might even be in his hand. Then, from nearly a half a century later, there is the splendid gem of a perspective by Frank Lloyd Wright – actually, this would have been done by a perspective artist in *his* office – of the Johnson Wax building (cat. 32).

Another Chicago connection within Barbara Pine's collection is a drawing by Louis Sullivan, very much in his big looping hand, a sketch design for the Babson House (cat. 2) that ties in with the Niedecken chair design made for Frank Lloyd Wright's Coonley House (cat. 5). Alongside the fact that Wright was now rivalling his former boss, both houses were built at the same time, close to one another in the Chicago suburb of Riverside. This has led architectural critics both then and now to make comparisons between the pair of houses and their architects.

Barbara Pine also holds a group of drawings by Ludwig Mies van der Rohe, the Bauhaus architect who finally came to live in Chicago in 1938, teaching at the Illinois Institute of Technology (cats 28 & 29). His archive now resides with MoMA.

The Barbara Pine collection has a particularly strong selection from the interwar years. From the 1920s are classic examples of Art Deco by the leading French stylists, including a circular design for an intriguing room interior by Émile-Jacques Ruhlmann (cat. 11) and, from the fashionable decorators Süe et Mare, an *ensemblier* (cat. 16). Barbara Pine also has a pair of fine designs by Andre Arbus, which are not in the exhibition, for a bed in the shape of a sleigh as well as desk and matching chair. There is also a topographical drawing, one of the rare few in the collection: Barbara Pine prefers design drawings, in other words, to see the architects thinking, rather than views of their buildings after completion. But this charming and dense little gouache of the Pomone Pavilion at the Paris exposition of 1925 fits perfectly into the Art Deco theme (cat. 15).

There are certainly highlights from the major countries and architects associated with the rise of the Modern Movement. The great Le Corbusier, in an intimate moment, makes a design sketch for alterations to the lakeside villa he created for his parents and brother, one of his earliest works (cat. 26). From the Netherlands there is an important De Stijl work – showing that theoretical ideas can bear fruit – a collaborative effort between the architect Cornelis van Eesteren and the painter Theo van Doesburg, for a house that was built in 1923 (cat. 13). The impressive German contribution is of an icon of Expressionism, a drawing by Erich Mendelsohn for an interior in the Einstein Tower in Potsdam (cat. 12). And yet another first-rate Expressionist architect, Hans Poelzig with a fiery and fantastic stage design for his own Großes Schauspielhaus in Berlin (cat. 14). And, not to forget, the Mies van der Rohe drawings, including a design for a Mountain House (cat. 29) which had a strong influence upon a generation of architects after the Second World War.

From Sweden, Erik Gunnar Asplund working with his colleague Nils Einar Eriksson explores the Scandinavian approach at a critical moment of modernism during the Stockholm Exhibition of 1930 (cat. 24) and then, on his own, with a chair design which is considered a prototype for later developments (cat. 25).

Barbara Pine also delights in the Italian contribution. Although from just a year after the end of the Second World War, the drawing by Gio Ponti is in the neo-classical style of the architect's pre-war designs (cat. 34). Here is the most exquisite display cabinet, a confection of brilliance.

Much earlier, however, are the two drawings by Italian Futurist architects which are like manifestos, pronouncements of a new world of noisy speeding mechanised living. The Antonio Sant'Elia sketch is archetypal, rapid thoughts on monumental industrial buildings with streets almost in the clouds (cat. 7). And, from his acolyte Virgilio Marchi, a polished Futurist design demonstrating the dynamic forces of machine and electricity (cat. 23).

These Futurist works have much in common with the visionary drawings in the collection. Barbara Pine's Hermann Finsterlin drawing for one of his biomorphic buildings on a mountain top is not shown in this exhibition, but its science fiction world is not far removed from the Paolo Soleri design for a house, the 'Arizonian Nest', which looks like a flying saucer come to rest in the desert mountains (cat. 36). And the very name 'Dymaxion' given by Buckminster Fuller to his buildings as machines, evokes flights of invention exemplified in his rough drawing for a ten-deck house (cat. 20). Also included in this group is the Hugh Ferriss drawing of a view of the parabolic arched Municipal Asphalt Plant, New York, a building just completed when he drew it in about 1945 (cat. 33). As America's most famous architectural perspective artist, known for his visionary views of cities, most notably in his publication *The Metropolis of Tomorrow*

(1929), Ferriss's drawing in the Barbara Pine collection evokes the power and dark beauty of the new forms emerging in architecture.

The 1950s and '60s are represented by a few prime examples of drawing style and architectural excellence. The hard pencil work of Paul Rudolph recreates the raw energy of his Brutalist architecture in an unbuilt scheme for the major city buildings of New Haven, Connecticut (cat. 42). From Álvaro Siza, a telling sketch of his Boa Nova Tea House, a major twentieth-century building in the architect's native Portugal. And, a highlight of the collection – as if the collection didn't have enough already – a large study by Louis Kahn for the Inner Court of the Indian Institute of Management, Ahmedabad, India, in which the colourful and polished perspective is surrounded by a border of sketch ideas (cat. 37).

In terms of numbers, however, the strongest contingent of drawings in the Barbara Pine collection is for work from the past thirty years, especially by American architects. This corresponds with the length of time that Barbara Pine has been collecting, often personally visiting and getting to know the architects. As a result, examples of the many significant movements, the 'isms' that have recently shifted modern architecture, are here.

Befriending architects like Michael Graves and Frank Gehry just as their careers were taking off, accounts for such early Post-Modern designs as Graves's own house and the commemorative poster, respectfully signed to Barbara Pine by the architect, for his groundbreaking Portland Building, Oregon (cats 45 & 46). The sketches by Gehry all date from the early 1980s, a period of exploration for the architect before his big projects appeared, when he was composing chairs in cardboard, lighting fixtures in formica, and had the freedom to enter conjectural projects for invited exhibitions (cats 50, 51 & 52). Similarly, the housing design by Steven Holl was part of an invited project for exhibition, and was instrumental in laying the foundation for his later success (cat. 55).

Other drawings from American architects from this period include an electrifying competition design from 1980 by the young Billie Tsien and Tod Williams, another practice on the verge of gaining a respected career (cat. 48). And the concentrated power in the penmanship of Helmut Jahn as he methodically sketches ideas for skyscrapers (cat. 53). Seemingly out on a limb, yet really still part of this Post-Modern trend, is the outrageous design for an armchair by Peter Shire in a drawing which in its solid blocked colours captures the carnival atmosphere of the piece (cat. 49).

This witty and significant contribution to furniture by the Memphis Group seems not that far removed from the *armoire* in the shape of a cabana by the Italian Aldo Rossi (cat. 47). For Rossi, this drawing is central to his design philosophy, the cabana representing for him a very serious theoretical icon of the importance of place, the past and the possibilities of the future. Equally, the captivating charm of the coloured-up print of a housing unit by O.M. Ungers, speaks of a Post-Modern mentality of using classical or traditional forms clothed in modern dress (cat. 44).

Blowing these concepts apart are the drawings by the Deconstructivists. Paper allows theoreticians to explain their ideas, to simplify. Richard Meier reduces the geometric complexities of one of his early houses through the restricted lines of an axonometric projection (cat. 40). Daniel Libeskind, with a zigzag motion across the page expresses the tearing anguish innate in his design for the Jewish Museum in Berlin (cat. 58). Recalling a few intimate moments between architectural companions, Peter Eisenman's deconstructs before their eyes his latest theories and projects, in both unfolding image and broken phrases (cat. 56). And, from this millennium, Michael Maltzen deconstructs then reconstructs using the letters 'MoMA' as they break apart and then crunch up in a signboard over the museum's temporary quarters in Queens (cat. 60).

In these later drawings, we recognise that the art of drawing has not been lost in a design world dominated by the computer. That a poetic, thoughtful imagination can exist in direct representations on paper, from heart to mind to hand, is surely the essence of the Barbara Pine Collection.

The sizes of the drawings are given in millimetres: height precedes width

1 Dankmar Adler (1844–1900) & Louis Sullivan (1856–1924)

Design for the Auditorium Building, Chicago, Illinois, USA, c.1887

Transverse section through *Full Proscenium Opening 75'0"* & *Reduced Proscenium Opening 47'0"*
Scale: 3/64 inch to 1 foot
Inscribed: As above, *Chicago Auditorium Building* & details given
Signed: *Adler & Sullivan Architects*
Black & red pen on glazed linen (approx. 350 x 540)
Lit.: Joseph M. Siry, *The Chicago Auditorium Building: Adler and Sullivan's architecture and the city*. Chicago & London: University of Chicago Press, 2002

With a massive robust beauty, the Chicago Auditorium Building is a masterwork in late nineteenth-century American architecture that helped establish Chicago as a major world city. Behind its great masonry walls of granite and limestone, the architects Adler & Sullivan built a 400-room hotel, 136 offices and stores, and the tour de force, a theatre seating an audience of 4,200. So large was the project that it opened in stages between 1888 and 1890.

The design shows a cross-section through the auditorium and the adjoining tower, which marked the entrance to the theatre and is shown with the vertical opening of the elevator shaft serving only the upper floors. The major features of the auditorium are illustrated: the wide proscenium of the full stage with its series of great arches and the smaller, square reduced proscenium, required to be dropped into place so that most productions would not be overwhelmed by the size of the stage.

The interior of the auditorium, today still a glittering confectionary, was done out with the elliptical ceiling arches in gold leaf and oil, gilded stencilled patterns and studded with electric light bulbs. This was the decorative work of Louis Sullivan, whose stylised pattern of foliated cast plaster designs are picked out in the drawing. Adler was the theatre design specialist.

This is an office drawing, drawn on linen that has been glazed, more durable than paper, easy enough to be rolled and taken on to the building site. The young Frank Lloyd Wright was working in Adler & Sullivan's office at the time, and one of his tasks was to transfer Sullivan's sketches into construction drawings. Could this be one of them?

1

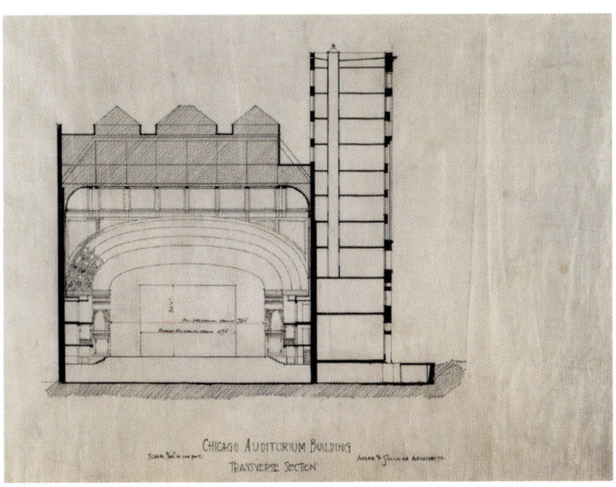

2 Louis Sullivan (1856–1924)

Preliminary design for the Henry Babson House, Riverside, Illinois, USA, c.1907

Sketch ground floor plan [ie. first floor in America] & two sketch front elevations
Inscribed: rooms labelled
Pencil on paper (approx. 840 x 510)
Lit.: Robert Twombly and Narciso G. Menocal, *Louis Sullivan: the poetry of architecture*. New York & London: Norton, 2000, reprd fig. 203; David van Zanten, *Sullivan's city: the meaning of ornament for Louis Sullivan*. New York & London: Norton, 2000; *Architectural Record*, Vol. 30, Oct. 1911, pp.326–338

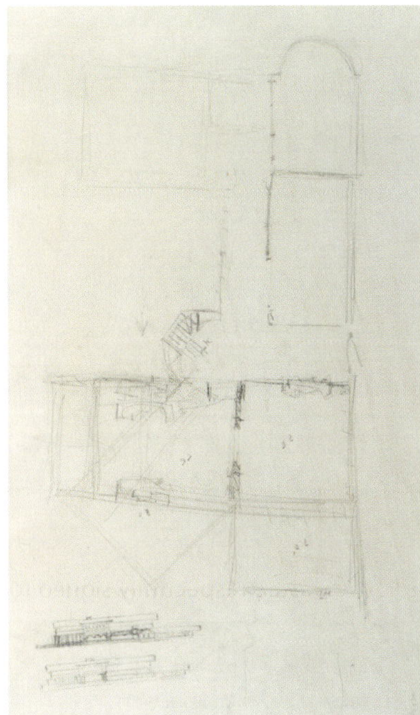

2

In this big rough sketch, the architect Louis Sullivan searches for a workable plan for a large suburban house. The Babson House is to be long, with projecting wings on the ground floor at right-angles on the rear elevation. Here Sullivan lightly and hesitantly sketches one wing overlaying another at 45 degrees to the body of the house, an idea he was to reject. The small protruding turret labelled 'stair' is the staircase. But the essence of the final built design is here. The axis of circulation on the ground floor is via a corridor-like gallery which joins the wings and the principal rooms.

In the little elevations, the series of arches on the first floor are perceptible. This is a sleeping balcony, and was built with characteristic Sullivanesque foliated ornamentation, with columns with a Moorish flavour.

By about 1907 when Sullivan created this design, his greatest years working with Dankmar Adler on some of Chicago's most famous office buildings were well and truly past. However, the Babson House proved to be the first of a trio of residences, followed soon after by the Bradley and Bennett Houses, which established Sullivan as a master of domestic planning. Coincidentally, the Babson House was built at the same time and located near to his former pupil Frank Lloyd Wright's Coonley House.

3 Koloman Moser (1868–1918)

Design for an *armoire* (wardrobe), *c*.1904

Front & side elevations with inset perspective
Inscribed: *190 hoch* [ie. 190cm high] / *2 strich* [ie. 2 lines]
Pen & pencil on graph paper (330 x 410)
Lit.: Antonio D'Auria and Daniele Baroni, *Kolo Moser, grafico e designer / Kolo Moser: graphic artist and designer*. New York: Rizzoli, 1984, photograph of *armoire*, p.127

An exemplary piece of furniture design of the Wiener Werkstätte by one of its leading exponents. Along with Josef Hoffman, Koloman Moser had founded the Wiener Werkstätte in 1904, a workshop and gallery in Vienna making furniture, textiles and objects that combined art and handicraft while attempting to reject historical influences. In style and practice, the Wiener Werkstätte was greatly influenced by Charles Rennie Mackintosh.

A favoured motif of both Mackintosh and the Wiener Werkstätte was setting dark squares on a white background. This *armoire* has just such a pattern: the whole a white box outlined in black lines and then with a short row of small checks painted on the top centre of each door.

Moser drew this design in freehand, rather than ruling the lines, an expression of the arts and crafts freedom within the Wiener Werkstätte movement. The *armoire* was executed almost as shown in this drawing: complete with its ball feet, the whole body painted and lacquered white with its attenuated black patterning.

3

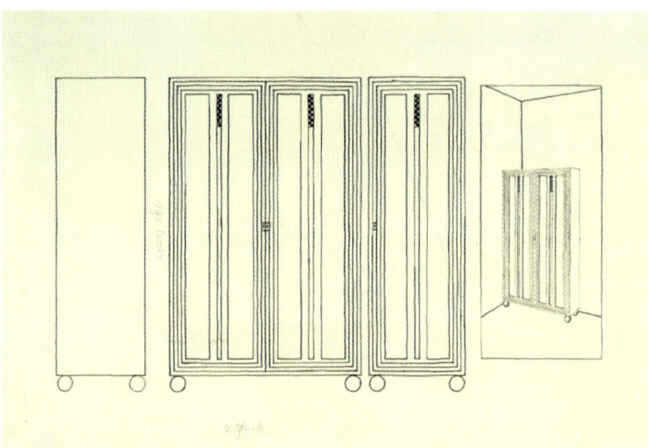

4 Charles Rennie Mackintosh (1868–1928)

Design for an easy chair, *c*.1905

Front & side elevations
Inscribed: *wood fillet at sides / leather*, also filed with the drawing a sheet with a note in the architect's hand: *To be made in oak / with leather seat & stuffed leather back*
Pencil & green wash on paper (approx. 175 x 145)
Lit.: Christie's (London) catalogue, *The Dr Thomas Howarth collection: important works by Charles Rennie Mackintosh, Margaret Francis McDonald and Herbert MacNair*, 17 Feb 1994, reprd fig.115; Roger Billcliffe, *Charles Rennie Mackintosh: the complete furniture, furniture drawings and interior designs*. London: J. Murray, 1986, 3rd edition, alternative design illustrated p.21, D1905

4

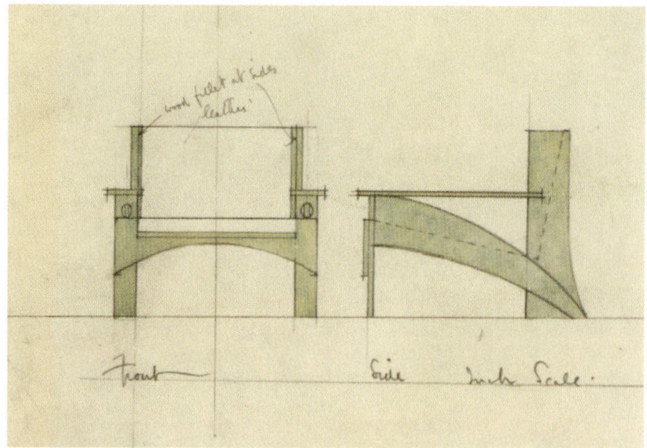

This is not a chair design one would at first sight associate with Charles Rennie Mackintosh, that great exponent of Scottish Art Nouveau. Where are the all too familiar characteristics of Mackintosh furniture that have made them such modern classics: the tall ladder back, the check pattern, the ebony black or glossy ivory finish, the stylised rose motif?

Here, however, is another facet to Mackintosh, one that is more architectural than decorative. This is not a chair for a silk-swathed lady to perch delicately upon in a Glasgow tea-room. Rather it is low, broad and tough, of oak and leather. With great curving arm-braces and a wide back profile which splays at the bottom, this is engineering, a pairing of flying and setback buttresses.

Nevertheless, Mackintosh retains his fondness for the right angle: this chair design is square in plan, cubic in form. Decoration is stripped, the only discreet embellishment being functional: on the front legs the oval shape is flush dowelling.

This chair design was not executed. (Detail only illustrated)

5 George Mann Niedecken (1878–1945)

Design for *hall chair*, Coonley House, Riverside, Illinois, USA, *c*.1908

Perspective
Inscribed: As above & *For Mr and Mrs Avery Coonley, Riverside, Illinois*
Signed: *Niedecken Walbridge Interior Architects*
Pen & coloured washes on tracing paper (approx. 255 x 105)
Lit.: Cheryl Robertson, *Frank Lloyd Wright and George Mann Niedecken: Prairie School collaborators*. Lexington, Mass.: Milwaukee Art Museum, 1999; Thomas A. Heinz, *Frank Lloyd Wright: interiors & furniture*. London: Academy Editions, 1994, preliminary design illustrated, p.122; *Architects' drawings from the collection of Barbara Pine*. Evanston, Illinois: Mary and Leigh Block Gallery, Northwestern University, 1987, p.32

Until recently, it was assumed that Frank Lloyd Wright was the sole designer of the furniture for his architectural projects. He often bragged of the fact. However, for at least eleven of his earlier commissions for houses in and around Chicago, Wright found a local collaborator in George Mann Niedecken.

Niedecken and his brother-in-law John Walbridge called themselves 'architect decorators', or as on this drawing, 'interior architects', implying that they could pick up on the stylistic language and harmonize with the overall architect of a given project. It is obvious from both the design of this hall chair and the style of the drawing, that Niedecken has absorbed Wright's

5

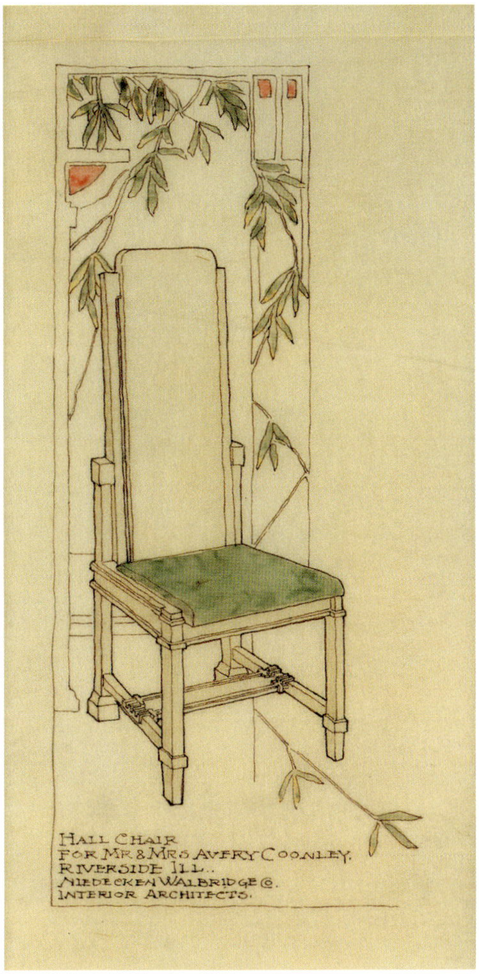

style. Typically, therefore, the chair itself is to be made in oak, with a tall flat back, squared structure and leather-covered seat. And with its willow decoration and little red squares, the drawing is based loosely upon Japanese woodblock prints of the nineteenth century, similar again to the way in which Frank Lloyd Wright presented his drawings.

Niedecken created a large group of furniture pieces for the Coonley House, one of Wright's major house commissions. However, of the surviving chairs from this project, the ones which are most similar to this Niedecken drawing are more austere, with the back board extending to the floor and the legs and railings free of joint decoration. In other words, it would appear that the architect modified Niedecken's design to make it more masculine and purer in form . . . more Frank Lloyd Wright.

6 Franz Schwarz (1887–?)

Student design for a Mausoleum for the Knights of the Order of Maria Theresa, *c.*1912

Plan & elevation
Scale: *Grundriss* [ie. floor plan] *1:800*
Inscribed: *Die Heldengrauft / für die Maria Theresien Ordensritter*
Pen & pencil on paper (440 x 345)
Lit.: *Architects' drawings from the collection of Barbara Pine.* Evanston, Illinois: Mary and Leigh Block Gallery, Northwestern University, 1987, p.39, reprd p.38

Franz Schwarz was a pupil of the architect Otto Wagner and this drawing appears to be a student project from Schwarz's period at the 'Wagnerschule', Wagner's master classes held at the Akademie für Bildenden Künste in Vienna. In style, this design exemplifies the shift taking place in the Wiener Sezession, the Vienna Secessionist movement of the period, away from the decorative and towards a more austere form of classicism. The plan of this design is square and topped by a cupola, like that of the most important of Secessionist masterpieces, the Secession Building in Vienna, from 1898, by Wagner's associate architect, J. M. Olbrich. But that was a highly stylized building, and this unornamented temple design by Schwarz follows Wagner's dictate that decoration be determined by form and structure. So, here, the pillars at the ground floor, acting like modern flying buttresses, along with the corresponding upper pilasters, operate as the main decorative feature.

Die Heldengrauft may be translated as the Tomb of the Heroes. The structure, therefore, was a conjectural project for a mausoleum for knights of the Maria Theresien Orden, an order of the Austro-Hungarian Empire established by Empress Maria Theresa in 1757 for senior military officers who had performed acts of exceptional valour. The last holder was admitted in 1931.

6

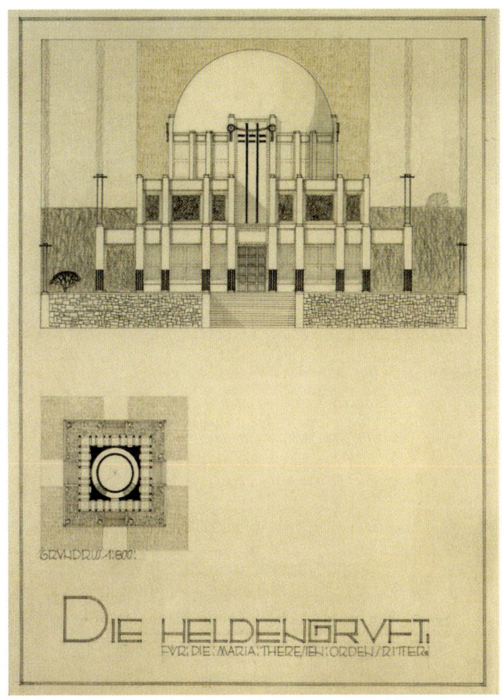

7 Antonio Sant'Elia (1888–1916)

Studies for buildings, *c.*1913

Inscribed: (in red pen) *28* & (estate stamp) *Arch. Antonio Sant'Elia / 30.4.1888- / 10.10.1916*
Pencil, black & red pen on paper (196 x 290)
Lit.: Luciano Caramel and Alberto Longatti, *Antonio Sant'Elia: the complete works.* New York: Rizzoli, 1988, reprd fig.25; *Antonio Sant'Elia: l'architecttura disegnata.* Catalogue of exhibition, Museo d'Arte Moderno di Ca' Pesaro, Venice, 1991, reprd p.173, fig.147; *Architects' drawings from the collection of Barbara Pine.* Evanston, Illinois: Mary and Leigh Block Gallery, Northwestern University, 1987, p.36

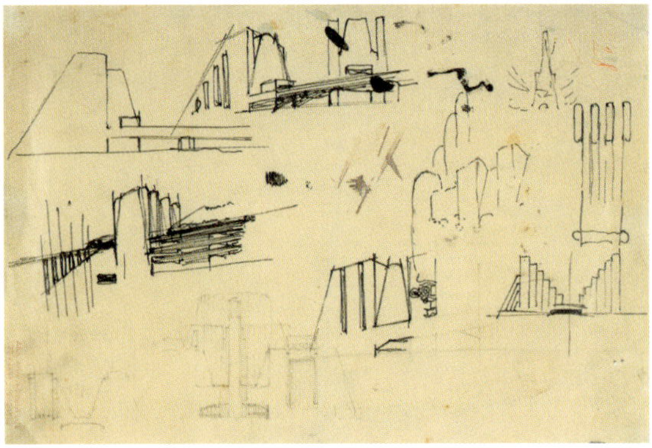

7

In only a few short years, between 1912 and 1915, Antonio Sant'Elia filled sketchbook after sketchbook, sheet after sheet, with his futuristic visions for a *Città Nouva*, a new city of monumental industrial and mechanised buildings. In 1915, he joined the Italian army and was killed the following year in battle, aged 28. Yet the drawings, and his 1914 manifesto on futuristic architecture, established Sant'Elia as the leading architect and one of the most influential members of the Futurist movement.

It is difficult to fathom exactly what type of structure or structures Sant'Elia is proposing in these frenetic but purposefully drawn sketches. The funnel profiles, rows of cylinders, moving gangways and pavements – 'oblique and elliptical lines are dynamic', he proclaimed in his manifesto – all these shapes relate to Sant'Elia's many designs for electrical power stations, factories, cathedrals, cityscapes. This is monolithic architecture, with beauty in its then perceived ugliness. It is noisy, anarchic but practicable; a Futurist city where aeroplanes can land on rooftops, buildings dive into the bowels of the earth, a place which, as Sant'Elia said, 'must soar up on the brink of a tumultuous abyss'.

8 Josef Hoffmann (1870–1956)

Design for an interior, 1917

Elevation
Scale: *M1:20*
Dated: *16 12 17*
Inscribed: (on a former mount) *Eingangsseite* [ie. entrance side]
Pencil, coloured washes & applied silver foil on graph paper
(305 x 310)
Lit.: Eduard F. Sekler, *Joseph Hoffmann, the architectural work: monograph and catalogue of works*. Princeton, N.J. & Guildford: Princeton University Press, 1985

In 1916 Josef Hoffmann collaborated with Eduard Wimmier, a colleague at the Wiener Werkstätte, in creating a fashion department for the company, opening a shop on Kärntnerstrasse in Vienna. Walls and furnishings were covered with wallpaper, stencilling and textiles in a foliage-and-blossom Wiener Werkstätte pattern.

A similar pattern of flowers-and-tendrils appears in this drawing for an unidentified interior designed by Hoffmann. In style, this interior has a distinctly Swedish Modern touch about it, with the wood panelling, reclining sculpture (beautifully worked on the drawing in silver foil), circular light fitting or window, and the long curving door handles. But as Hoffmann has dated the drawing 1917, this would indeed be an early manifestation of the look. This was the year that he worked on an exhibition of

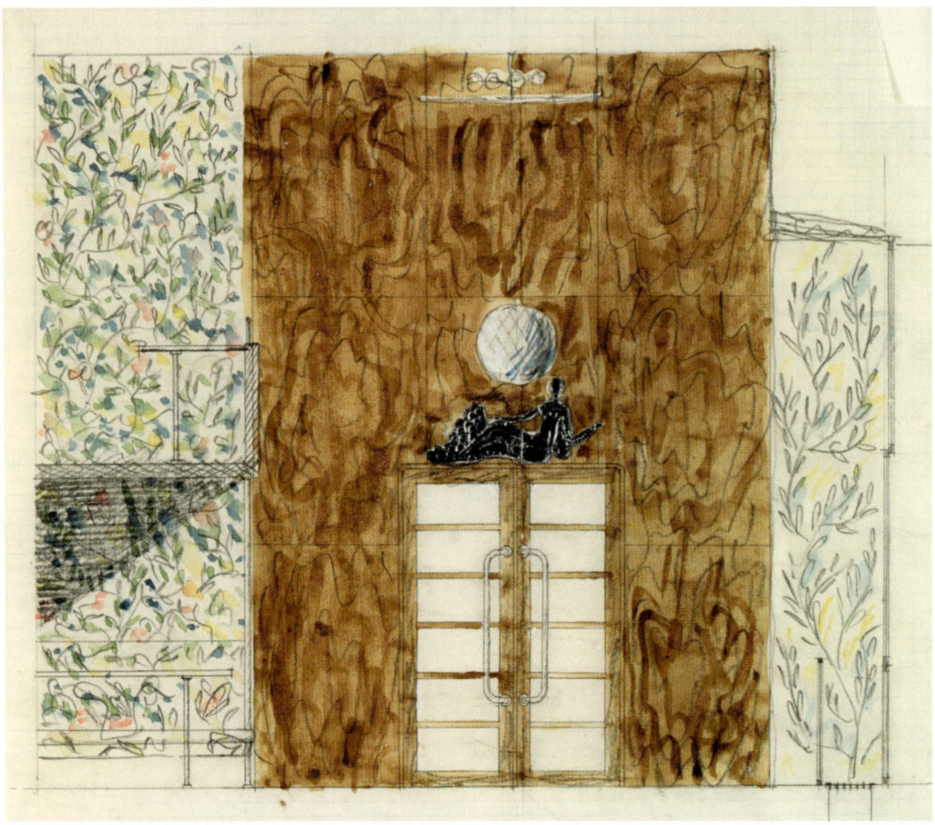

8

Austrian design which was shown at the newly built Liljevalch Konsthall in Stockholm, Sweden; but this does not seem to match the gallery interiors by Carl Bergsten. In addition, there is a balcony in this design, and a handrail at ground level. Hoffmann was working on many projects at the time: this interior, therefore, could possibly be for an exhibition pavilion or a branch of the Wiener Werkstätte in another city.

9 Josef Hoffmann (1870–1956)

Design for architect's own 1933 Christmas card, *c.*1932, with printed card with pen inscription from the architect, *c.*1950

Inscribed: (Christmas card) *Die Allerherzli / Chstenwüsche / zuweihnachtund / Neujahr / senpen / Josef und Caria / Hoffmann / 1933* [ie. The most heartfelt good wishes for Christmas and the New Year are sent by Josef and Caria Hoffmann, 1933] & (printed card) *W . . .* [illegible] *vielen dank für alles Gute und viele Wünsche für 1951 Ihre Josef Hoffmann* [ie. I wish to send many thanks and all good wishes for 1951. Yours, Josef Hoffmann]
Signed & dated: (Christmas card) as above & (printed card, in printed silver block letters) *JH*
(Christmas card) Pencil & coloured pencil on card (134 x 89) & printed card with pen added (open, 162 x 192)
Lit.: Eduard F. Sekler, *Joseph Hoffmann, the architectural work: monograph and catalogue of works*. Princeton, N.J. & Guildford: Princeton University Press, 1985
Not illustrated

Here is a double-barrelled prize: two items of design ephemera by Josef Hoffman. The earliest is his personal Christmas card design for 1933. The illustration is a tall Christmas tree, topped by a star, flanked at the wavy base by a reclining figure and what appears to be a dog. The elongated tree has a loose association with the exhibition that Hoffmann was working on at the time, 'Fifty years of the Viennese Association for Arts and Crafts', which featured as its focal point a tall pillar with an angel figure at its pinnacle.

The card is signed from Hoffmann and his much younger second wife, Caria, whom he had married in 1925, having met her when she was a model in the fashion department of the Wiener Werkstätt, the studio shop for which he was a founder-designer.

The second item is also a card, made probably in late 1950, sending the earlier card to an unknown recipient with good wishes for 1951. It folds out, with the outer side printed with a pattern no doubt by Hoffman, and a red interior with two white squares on either side: within the one on the left are the stylized initials of Josef Hoffmann printed in silver, and within the one on the right, the architect's dedication.

10 Josef Hoffmann (1870–1956)

Alternative designs for a bentwood chair, *c.*1935

Elevations and perspective
Inscribed: (verso) *Sitzmöbel aus geschr* [illegible] *Holz, . . .* [illegible] [ie. wood seating furniture made from . . . wood . . .] & (signed) *Josef Hoffmann*
Signed: (recto) *JH*
Pen & wash on graph paper (205 x 145)
Lit.: Christopher Wilk, 'Furnishing the future: bent wood and metal furniture, 1925–1946' in Derek E. Ostergard ed., *Bent wood and metal furniture*. New York: University of Washington Press, 1987, pp.121–73

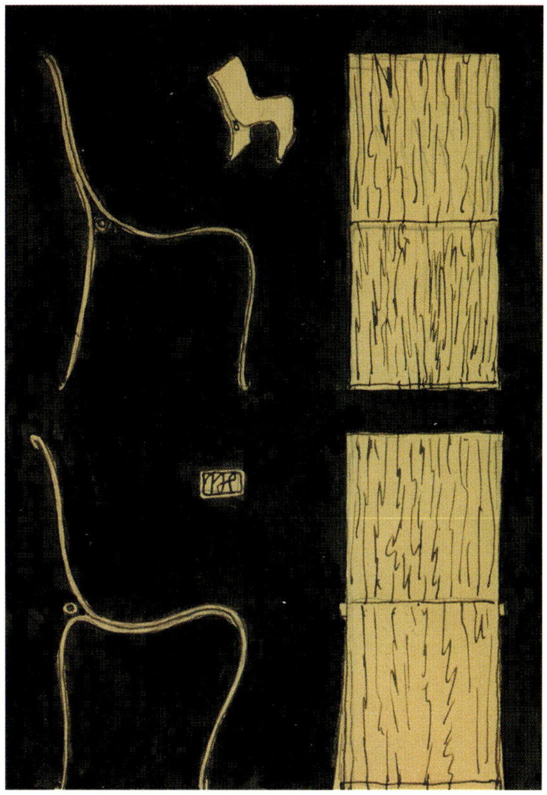

10

Josef Hoffmann created many classic bentwood chairs from as early as around 1900, some of which are still in production today. But all those designs were based on the bentwood as a frame. In this design, made much later in Hoffmann's career, the architect is reacting to the new innovations in bending sheets of plywood being made by fellow architect-furniture designers like Alvar Aalto and Marcel Breuer.

Both chair designs in this drawing act upon the principle of two overlapping sheets of moulded plywood strengthened, presumably by a metal rod, at the weakest joint where the back meets the rear support. The overlap in the top chair takes place on the back, and on the bottom chair with the seat. Although the concept is highly original, neither chair went into production

This is a typically striking drawing by Hoffmann from his later period, made on graph paper, with the images set dramatically against a black washed background, rather in imitation of a blueprint. The designer's stylized initials appear in a little box, like a sterling mark on a piece of silver.

11 Émile-Jacques Ruhlmann (1879–1933)

Circular design for a study with built-in daybed with bookcase, *c.*1918

Perspective
Pencil, pen & coloured crayons on buff paper (circular diameter 223, within double line border, on mount 330 x 250)

Ruhlmann was France's premier designer in the Art Deco period. His furniture was sophisticated in its simplicity and rich in opulent materials like his favourite macassar ebony and amboyna burl.

This drawing is strikingly similar, in style and technique, to the selection of design drawings made between 1913 and 1924 which

11

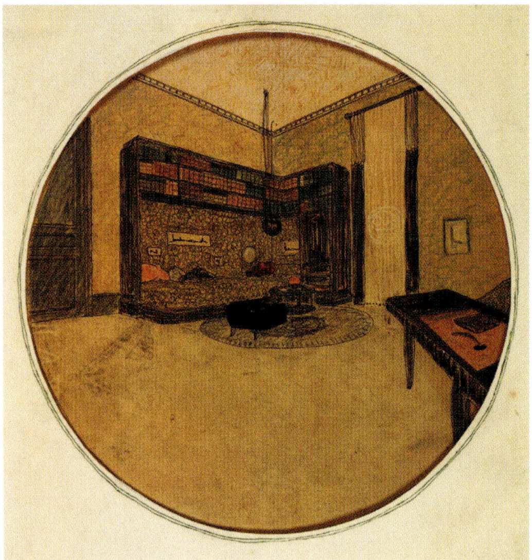

Ruhlmann published in his book *Harmonies*. Typical of his drawing style is the swirling line on carpets, furnishings, even walls and ceilings.

The setting here would appear to be a study in a large apartment, with a Ruhlmannesque desk on slender pointed legs. The focus, however, is the magnificent, and unique, freestanding unit which combines a sofa-daybed with a bookcase. In *Harmonies*, the designer illustrated a seating banquette within a niche, and like this drawing, combined it with the very same circular occasional table set on a round carpet. Another similarity is that both the published design and this drawing are circular.

12 Eric Mendelsohn (1887–1953)

Design for workroom, Einstein Tower, Potsdam, Germany, *c.*1920

Elevation
Black, green & red crayon on paper (approx. 160 x 160)
Lit.: Klaus Hentschel, *Der Einstein-Turm*. Berlin & New York: Spektrum, 1992; 'Organic! Einstein, Finlay-Freundlich, Mendelsohn, and the Einstein Tower in Potsdam' in Regina Stephan ed., *Erich Mendelsohn: architect 1887–1953*. New York: Monacelli, 1999, pp.26–37

12

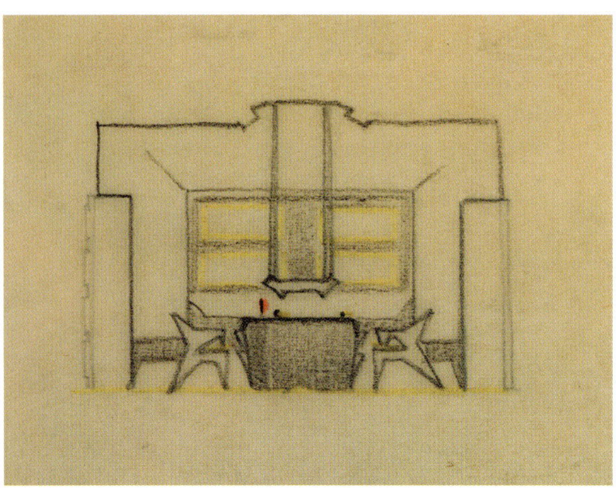

This is a rare find: a Mendelsohn design for one of the rooms in the Einstein Tower. The fluid, almost melting shape of the exterior of the building is an icon of the German Expressionist movement, well-known through other drawings by the architect and many photographic images. And, the building still survives.

But the interior is less documented. From an extant photograph of this workroom just after the Tower was finished in 1921, and also as the table and chairs still survive *in situ*, we know that the design in this drawing is very close to that executed. As built, the chairs were less angular and spiky, and the table has legs. The suspended overhead lamp has now disappeared. And, architecturally, the windows have rounded edges, in keeping with the dissolving sculptural form of the building.

The Einstein Tower was created as a research laboratory for a foundation dedicated to explore Albert Einstein's new and controversial General Theory of Relativity, based on mass and energy. Mendelsohn worked Einstein's Theory into his building programme, believing that the architectural mass could overcome the energy, ie. gravity. The tower was topped by an observatory cupola with mirrors to capture the light of the sun, moon or stars, which was then deflected down to the laboratory below ground. The workroom, on ground level, along with the adjoining small room for night accommodation, were the only two rooms in the building furnished by Mendelsohn.

13 Cornelis van Eesteren (1897–1988) & Theo van Doesburg (1883–1931)

Design for Mrs Van Zessen's house, 89 West Kinderdijk, Alblasserdam, Netherlands, 1923

Site plan, section & elevations
Scale: Site plan, given *1:100* [here 1cm = 2m]; section & elevations, given *1:200* [here 1cm = 1m]
Inscribed: *Woonhuis Te Alblasserdam / Petite Maison À Alblasserdam*
Signed: *C. van Eestern architecte / Théo van Doesburg peintre*
Print with coloured washes & gouache added on paper (370 x 488)
Lit.: *Architects' drawings from the collection of Barbara Pine*. Evanston, Illinois: Mary and Leigh Block Gallery, Northwestern University, 1987, p.44, reprd p.45; Els Hoek ed., *Theo van Doesburg: oeuvre catalogue*. Utrecht: Centraal Museum, 2000

This is a collaborative design between the architect Cornelis van Eesteren and Theo van Doesburg, painter, art theoretician and a leading spokesman for De Stijl, the movement which attempted a rational and geometric approach to art and architecture, somewhat similar to the Bauhaus of the same period. This small brick house, backing on to a canal, was designed and built for the widow Mrs Van Zessen in Van Eesteren's native town of Alblasserdam. At the time, Van Eesteren and Van Doesburg were working on their manifestos *Tot een beeldende architectuur* (Towards a plastic architecture) and *Vers une construction collective* which expounded their theory on colour and architecture. Thus the wooden window frames, shutter and doors have been hand-coloured on this print to define space and volume, as for example: red = height, yellow = length, blue = width. It is all like a painting by Piet Mondrian, another leader of the De Stijl. In 1924, Van Eesteren wrote to Van Doesburg, 'The colours of Mrs Van Zessen's house are lovely. I see it every day and take fresh pleasure in it every time' (letter in Netherlands Office for Fine Arts, The Hague).

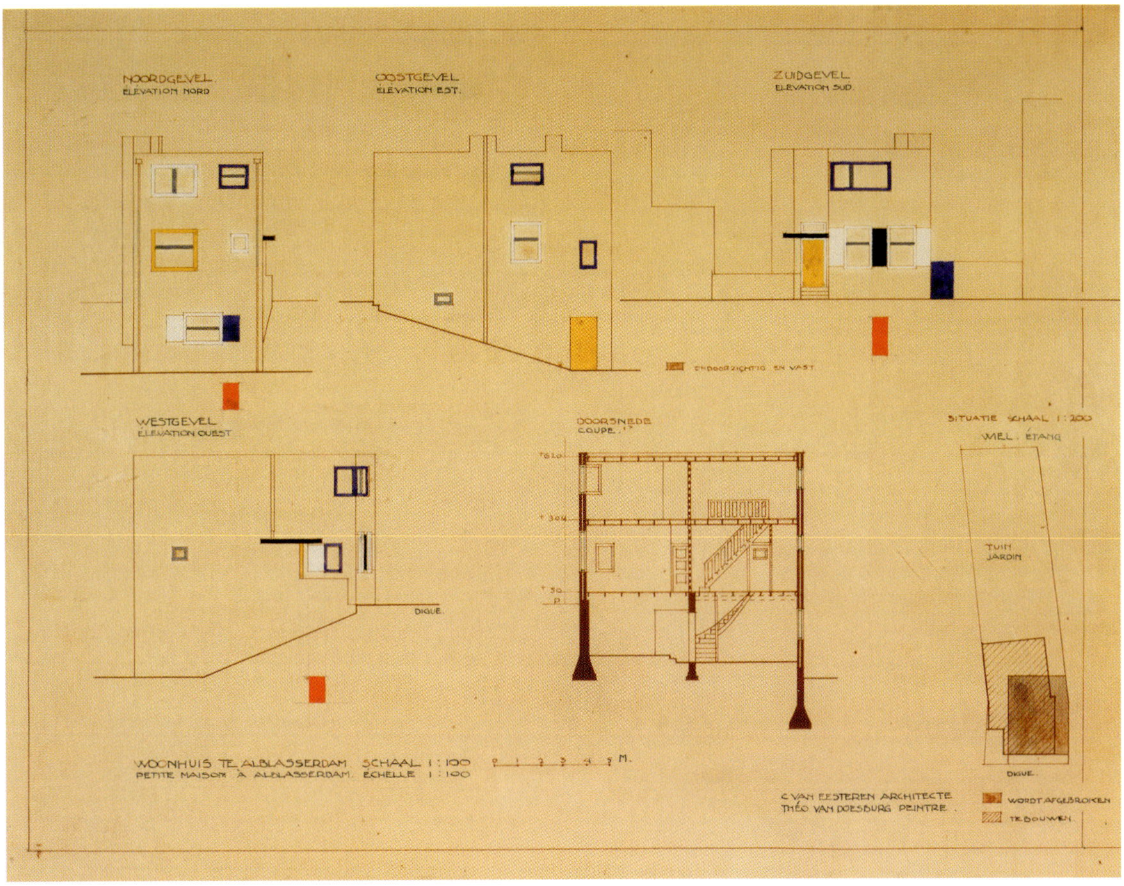

13

14 Hans Poelzig (1869–1936)

Studies for capitals & stage set design for *King Lear*, both for the Großes Schauspielhaus, Berlin, Germany, *c.*1923

Coloured pastel on paper (325 x 253)
Lit.: Christian Marquart, *Hans Poelzig: Architect, Maler, Zeichner / architect, painter, designer*. Tubingen: Wasmuth, 1995; *Der Dramatische Raum: Hans Poelzig: Malerei, Theater, Film*. Krefeld: Krefelder Kunstmuseen, 1986

This is an exquisite drawing – and one difficult to interpret. In 1918–19, Poelzig had designed and built the Großes Schauspielhaus, the Grand Playhouse of Berlin, a highpoint of the German Expressionist movement; with its organic auditorium dripping with plaster ornamentation it had earned the appropriate nickname of 'the stalactite cave'.

The foyer of the theatre, however, had weighty columns, topped by unique capitals. In fact, they were in the shape of the three shallow mushroom profiles Poelzig has sketched at the top of this drawing. But these could not be designs for these capitals, as this drawing is after the fact; they are rather more a fond recollection by the architect of the theatre in which, at the moment of this drawing, he was creating stage sets for a production of Shakespeare's *King Lear*.

The fiery strokes of colour in the two rows below are elevations of the *King Lear* stage set. Although seemingly abstract, the lines probably represent coloured lights, flooding the surfaces of the backdrops. Judging by corresponding drawings for this stage design in other collections, in the top elevation, the blue at the lower section of the centre section corresponds to a steep grand staircase down which the tragic figure of King Lear was to make his entrance. Cutting across the drawing, between capitals and elevations, is a thin plan showing the shallow U-shape of the stage set.

The production, however, never took place. And as for Poelzig's Großes Schauspielhaus, it was left to deteriorate in the former East Germany, quietly disappearing during the mid-1980s, just before German unification.

15 Unidentified early twentieth-century artist

View of the Pomone Pavilion for the Grand Magasins du Bon Marché, at the Exposition des Arts Décoratifs Modernes, Paris, France, *c.*1925

Exterior view
Gouache & watercolour on paper within painted border (245 x 388)

The density of the gouache paint gives a luminous sheen to this night view of one of the prettiest little pavilions at the 1925 Paris exhibition, the Pomone Pavilion for the large Parisian department store Au Bon Marché. In the distance is the Eiffel Tower, tipped

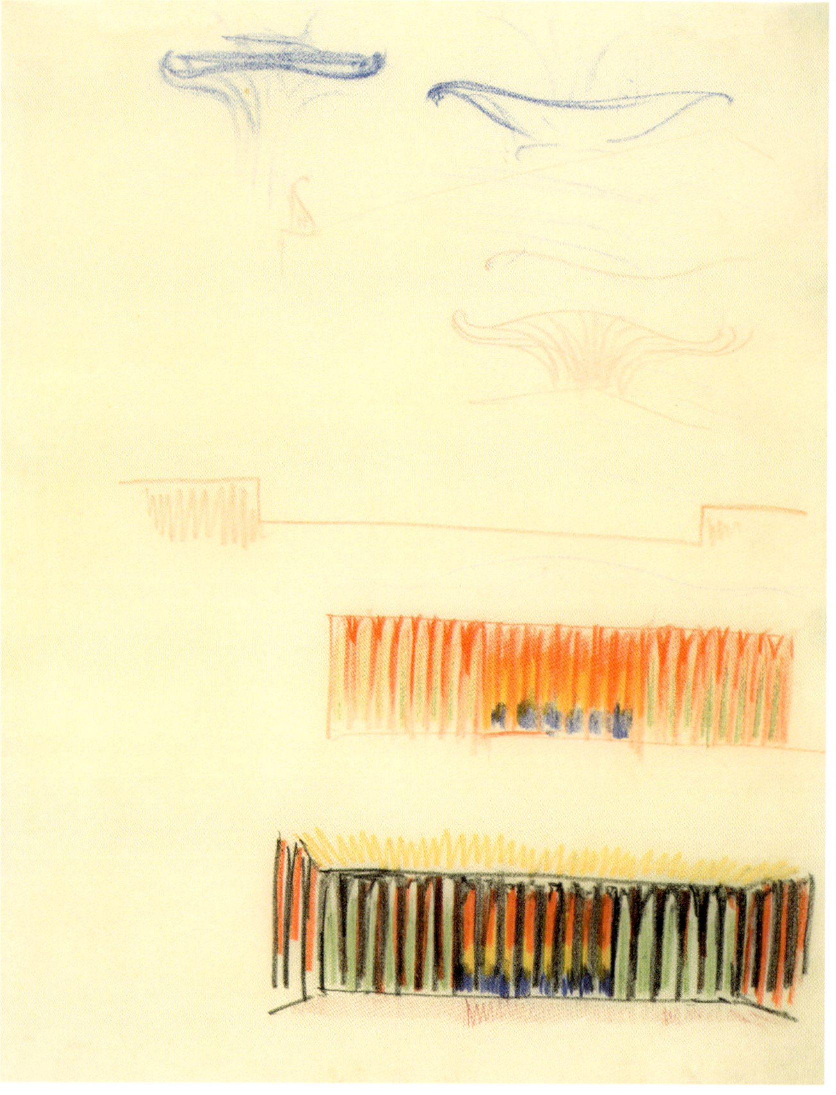

14

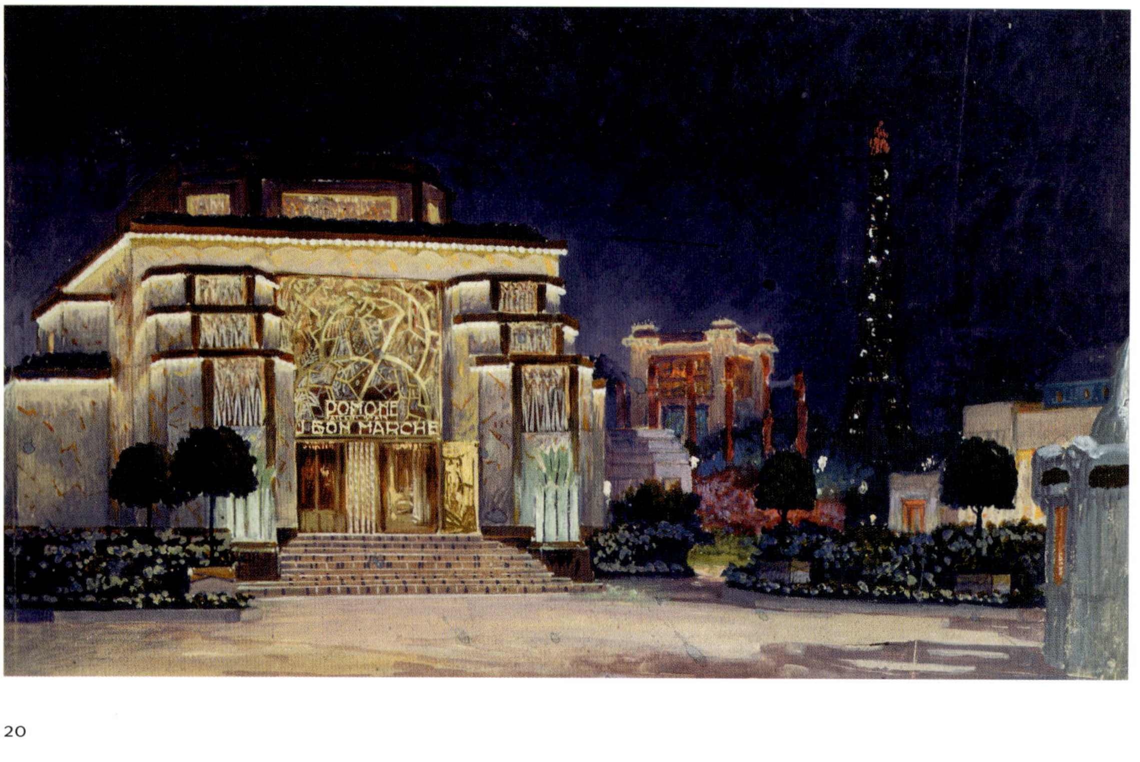

15

with the red of the newly erected illuminated sign of the car maker Citroën.

Pomone was the name of the art-furnishing section at Au Bon Marché, set up in 1923 under the artistic direction of one of France's premier decorator-designers, Paul Follot. A master of Art Nouveau, Follot moved gracefully into French Art Deco, a style whose very name derives from this famous exhibition. Follot's interior rooms of the Pomone Pavilion were much admired, and still are through photographs, with a grand salon, dining-room, smoking room, lady's boudoir – all in the newly fashionable richness and angularity of the new style.

The Pomone Pavilion was designed by the architect Louis-Hippolyte Boileu (1878–1948) and was set prominently at the beginning of the grand avenue to the 1925 Exposition at the foot of the Pont Alexandre III, near the river Seine. For the Exposition of 1937, Boileu working with the architects Carlu and Azéma, designed the Palais Chaillot, another great Art Deco pavilion which today still dominates the view across the Seine from the Eiffel Tower.

16 Louis Süe (1875–1968) & André Mare (1887–1932)

Design for the interior of a room, *c.*1925

Elevation
Inscribed: (stamped) *Compagnie / des Arts Français / 116 Faubg. St Honore / Paris* & *25*
Pencil, coloured washes & gold paint on paper (approx. 340 x 380)
Lit.: Florence Camard, *Süe et Mare et la Compagnie des Arts Français*. Paris: Les Éditions de l'Amateur, 1993

Süe et Mare founded the decorating company of the Compagnie des Arts Français in 1919, specialising in creating *ensembliers*, complete room settings. The *ensembliers* which Süe et Mare created at the 1925 Exposition des Arts Décoratifs Modernes in Paris brought them international recognition.

Although their firm continued until 1959, Süe et Mare left in 1928. This undated drawing, therefore, was made sometime in the 1920s. But, more pointedly, this is obviously an Art Deco design from the years around the Exposition. Typical of Süe et Mare, this design is not of a pure simplicity found in other great French Art Deco masters, like Émile-Jacques Ruhlmann, but mixes the new

16

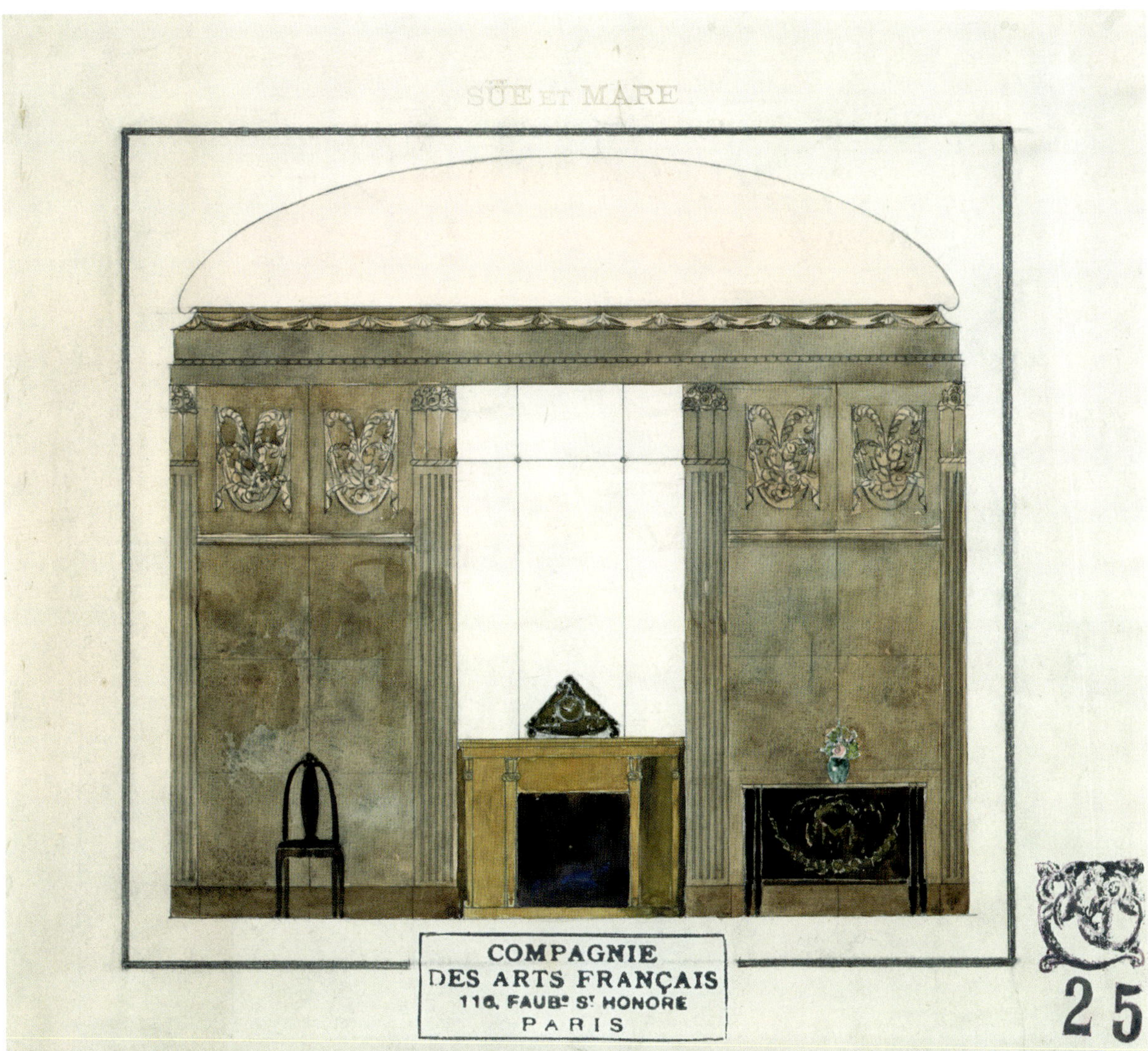

style with eighteenth-century fashions: the chair on the right is thoroughly modern, the commode on the left hints at revivalism. With a communal workshop of specialists like glassmakers, painters and ironworkers, Süe et Mare were able to draw upon craftsmen to create such showpieces as their favourite design for a triangular mantelpiece clock.

17 Eileen Gray (1878–1976)

Design for the *Centimetré* rug for the architect's own house, E1027, Cap Martin, Roquebrune, France, *c.*1925

Pen, gouache & coloured washes on paper (180 x 155)
Lit.: Peter Adam, *Eileen Gray: architect, designer: a biography*. London: Thames & Hudson, 2000, reprd p.183: Philippe Garner, *Eileen Gray 1878–1976: design and architecture*. Koln: Taschen, 1993, alternative design illustrated p.134

The *Centimetré* rug always appears prominently in photographs of the famous living room of Eileen Gray's French villa on the Côte d'Azur. Its ruled lines of markings make reference to Eileen Gray's profession as an architect . . . in fact, her new profession, because her villa was her first substantial work. To create the house, she had learned how to draw architecturally, which was different from making her more usual furniture and rug designs. Perhaps it was hard to get the metric scale out of her mind. Moreover, it reinforced the regulating, mechanistic aesthetic of the villa's modernism.

As made, the rug was very similar to the design in this drawing. However, the four scales were abridged to three, the numbers omitted on the scales and reduced along the edge, probably because of the difficulty of weaving these figures in wool. Also, a border line, like a ruler, was added along one edge. The number '10' was moved off the scale.

The *Centimetré* rug was woven in a dark blue, the colour of the sea.

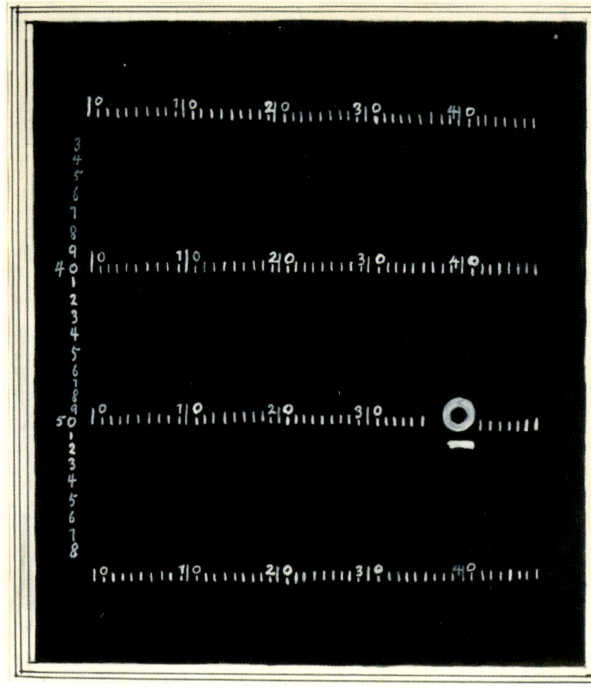

17

18 Eileen Gray (1878–1976)

Design for the *Marine d'Abord* rug for the architect's own house, E1027, Cap Martin, Roquebrune, France, *c.*1925

Pencil, blue & black washes, gouache, brown paper with collage on paper (100 x 225)
Lit.: *Architects' drawings from the collection of Barbara Pine*. Evanston, Illinois: Mary and Leigh Block Gallery, Northwestern University, 1987, p.44, reprd p.45; Caroline Constant, *Eileen Gray*. London: Phaidon, 2000, reprd p.102

18

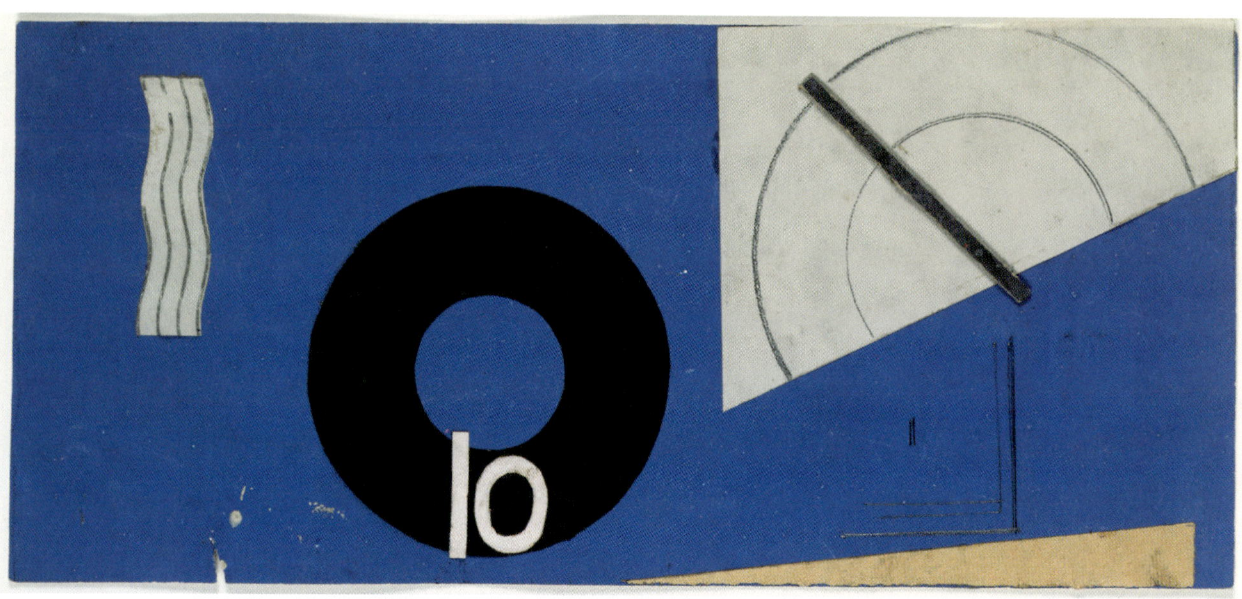

Eileen Gray began producing rugs in the early 1920s. These were sold alongside her furniture in her shop Jean Désert on rue du Faubourg Saint-Honoré in Paris. Under the direction of her friend Evelyn Wyld, she had a small team of weavers making up her designs.

This drawing is a little abstract painting, like a Cubist collage by Picasso or Braque. It is the final design for a rug that was made for Eileen Gray's own seaside villa, the oddly named E1027. This house was designed in association with Gray's friend, Jean Badovici, a Parisian-based Romanian architect and architectural writer, who advised on the technical aspects. Gray and Badovici shared use of the house, and after their relationship ended, he stayed on in the villa while she went on to build another house for herself.

The name E1027, through a combination of letters and numbers representing letters, denotes this collaboration by the couple's initials: E = Eileen, 10 = the tenth letter in the alphabet being J is for John, 2 = B, and 7 = G. So the number 10 on this rug, and also the *Centimetré* rug, is in homage to Jean Badovici.

19 Louis Brachet (1877–?)

Design for a kiosk, 1927

Perspective
Gouache & watercolour on paper (approx. 340 x 325)
Lit.: Louis Brachet, *L'architecture d'aujourd'hui: les rechereches de Louis Brachet*. Strasbourg, c.1932; *Architects' drawings from the collection of Barbara Pine*. Evanston, Illinois: Mary and Leigh Block Gallery, Northwestern University, 1987, reprd p.15

In this dark but intensely luminous watercolour, two chattering French flappers scurry along the boulevard. A gentleman, his umbrella tucked under his arm, placidly watches the world go by. It is such an appropriately light-hearted scene for a jolly little building.

Louis Brachet was a Parisian architect who came into his own about the time of this drawing, designing in a distinctive Art Deco style with a robust character. He was responsible for a Parisian hotel, a Dominican monastery, and a number of train stations, including the Gare de la Cité Universitaire and the Gare de

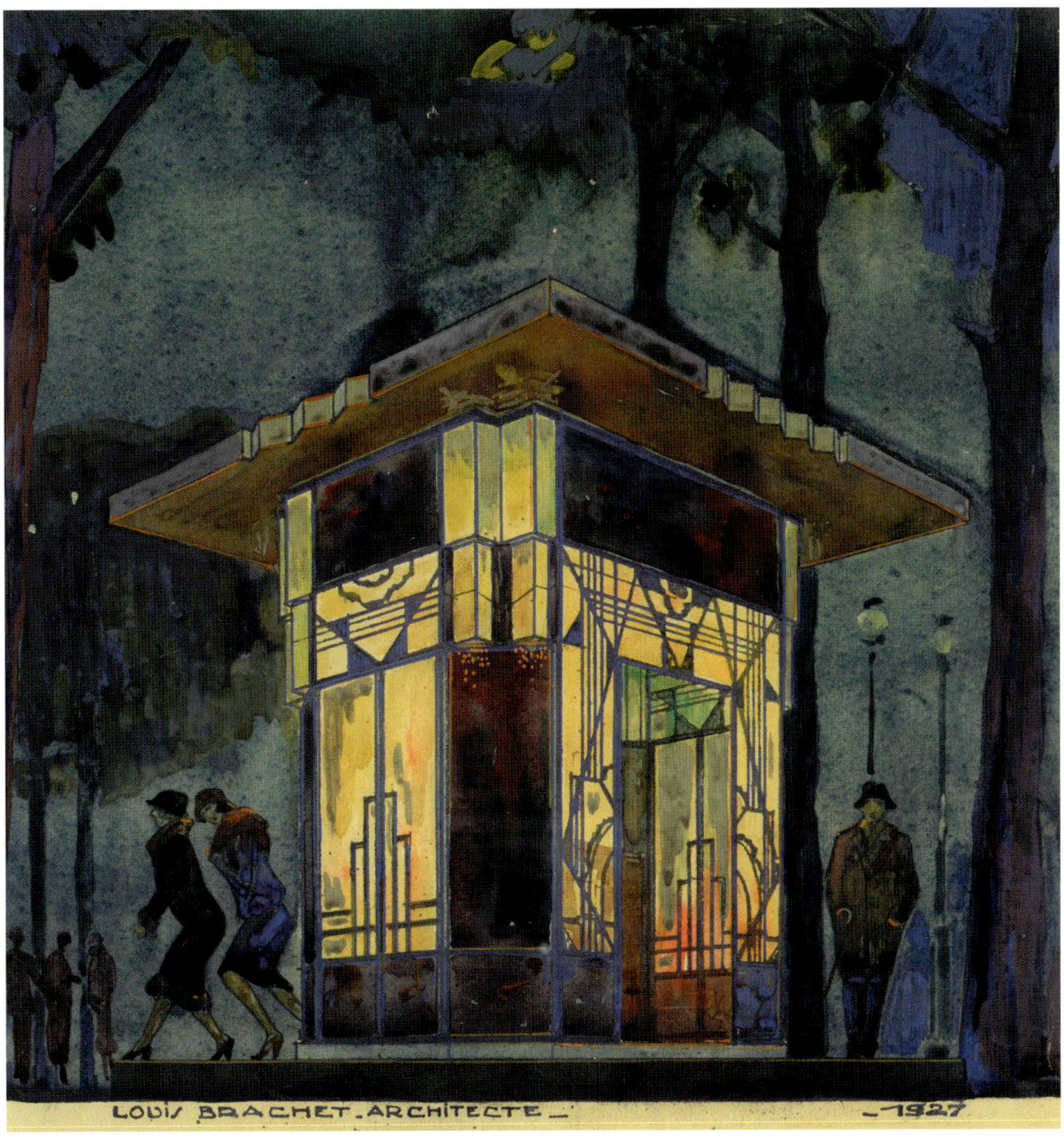

19

Gentilly, both in Paris, and the Gare de Neris-les-Bains in the Massif Central spa town. His Gare de Capdenac in the Lot, from the year after this drawing, has a broad clock tower roof with a zigzag edging similar to that of this kiosk.

The kiosk could be a transport shelter, or more likely, a magazine or tobacconist shop. Such little, illuminated buildings became popular in the 1920s in large European cities like Paris and Berlin, when the architectural effects of glass and lighting were finding new expressions.

20 R. Buckminster Fuller (1895–1983)

Study for the Ten-Deck House, *c.*1927

Aerial perspective
Pencil on tracing paper (275 x 200)
Lit.: R. Buckminster Fuller, *The artefacts of R. Buckminster Fuller: a comprehensive collection of his designs and drawings. Vol. I: The Dymaxion Experiment, 1926-1943.* New York: Garland, 1985, reprd p.15

This is an intriguing drawing by the high priest of the geodesic dome, Buckminster Fuller. But Fuller did not explore the geodesic until the 1940s. Rather, this drawing dates from his very first studies, the creation of his 4D Concept, 'four-dimensional thinking' as he referred to his investigations into mass production housing.

Fuller dubbed his futuristic houses of the period 'Dymaxion', a play on dynamic + maximum + ion, meaning tension. This design is for ten Dymaxion houses stacked one upon the other to form a tower. The houses, in this case the tower, are hung off a central column or mast used for supplying services like electricity and heating. The whole structure is stabilised by the tension of the criss-crossing cables. And it was supposedly so lightweight that it could be delivered by air, by a dirigible, and dropped into a hole in the ground, like planting a tree.

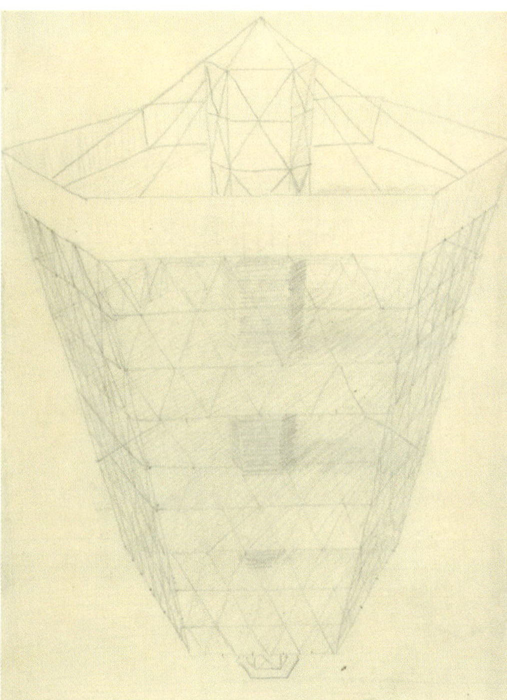

20

21 J. Roggen (*fl.*1929)

Design for the Choux House, Koekelberg, Brussels, Belgium, 1929

Elevation
Inscribed: *Propriete de Monsieur Choux / Rue François Hellinckx a / Koekelberg*
Signed & dated: *Bruxelles, Juin 1929 / L'Architecte: J. Roggen*
Pen, pencil, gouache & coloured washes on grey paper (430 x 370)
Lit.: *Architects' drawings from the collection of Barbara Pine.* Evanston, Illinois: Mary and Leigh Block Gallery, Northwestern University, 1987, p.34, reprd p.33

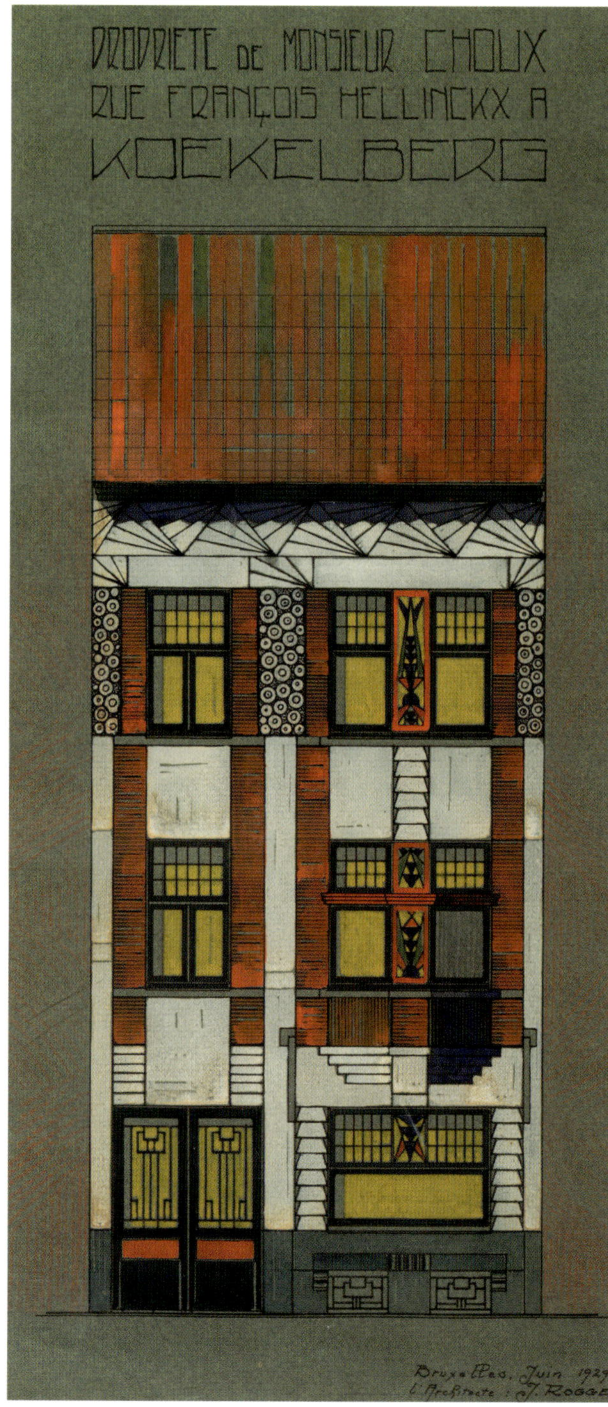

21

Many of the narrow house fronts in Belgium look like tapestries: ornamental, of bewildering patterns and mixed materials. The most famous period for these decorated façades was around 1900, at the height of Art Nouveau, led by such architects as Victor Horta. But the tradition continued on, and in the late 1920s and 1930s, Art Deco and streamlined modern styles were widely exploited.

This jewel of a drawing is for a house front in a suburb of Brussels. Drawn on dark paper, the windows are aglow with light to create a night view. The design is a lively assembly of jagged and circular forms in exposed brick, white stucco and tiles.

The architect, who here signs himself *J. Roggen* of Brussels, is a bit of a mystery. Another similar type of house façade design, made a few months later than this drawing, is held by the University of Pennsylvania Architectural Archive. Previously these drawings were attributed to Johannes Matthews Graadt van Roggen (1867–1959), but he was a deaf mute Dutch artist, not a Brussels architect.

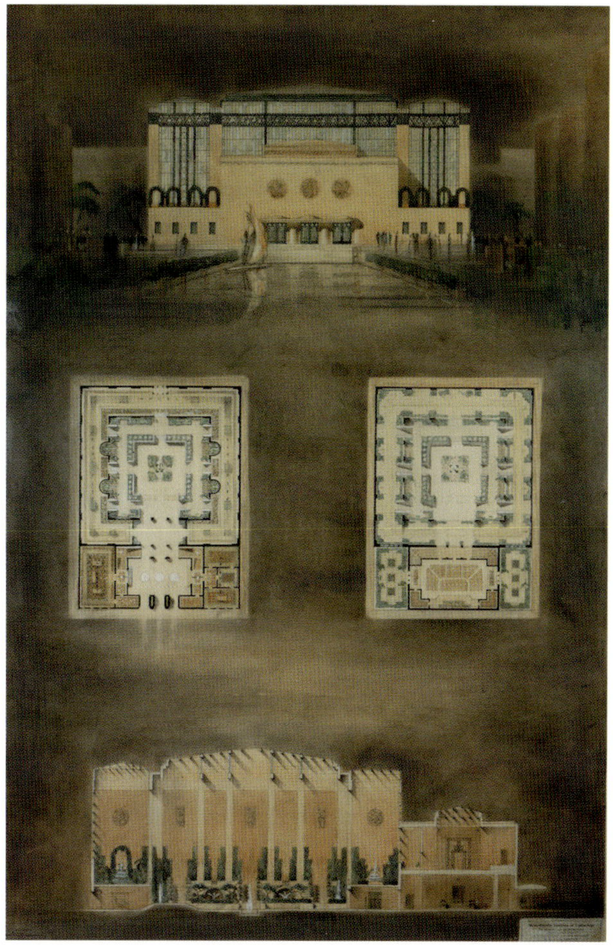

22

22 Mary Ann Elizabeth Crawford (1901–1988)

Student design for a *Horticultural Society Building*, *c.*1929

Plans, longitudinal section & perspective
Inscribed: As above & (on printed and typed attached label) *Massachusetts Institute of Technology / Department of Architecture / Class A - II Projet*
Signed: (on label) *M.A.E. Crawford*
Pen, brown crayon, white gouache, charcoal & coloured washes on paper (1380 x 940)
Lit.: Interview with M.A.E. Crawford, 17 May 1983, Chicago Architects Oral Interview Project, Art Institute of Chicago, Libraries & Archives, online: www.artic.edu/aic/libraries/caohp/crawford.html; *Architects' drawings from the collection of Barbara Pine*. Evanston, Illinois: Mary and Leigh Block Gallery, Northwestern University, 1987, p.17, reprd p.16

Beaux Arts meets Art Deco in this student drawing for a multi-functional building for a horticultural society. It is by Mary Ann Crawford, an architectural student at the Massachusetts Institute of Technology, in Cambridge, Massachusetts, one of the few architectural schools in the United States at the time to admit women. MIT was still firmly in the grip of the French Beaux Arts tradition, which had held influence in American architectural schools (and thus on American architecture and town planning) since the late nineteenth century, although this was about to change radically with the introduction of the new Modernism of the Bauhaus.

Typical of the Beaux Arts school of architectural draughtsmanship, Crawford's drawing for this 'projet' (as the label indicates in French) is formal, precise, symmetrical and beautiful – like the architecture itself. The two plans show an interior dominated by a glass-enclosed hall with complex spaces of multi-levels, steps, fountains, avenues and enclosures; the periphery is set aside for 'model exhibitions'. Although classical and rigorous, the Beaux Arts still allowed for a liberal spirit like Crawford's to adapt elements of the new Art Deco style: large rounded sculpture and the trademark zigzag patterns.

Upon graduating in 1929, Mary Ann Crawford obtained her Master's degree in architecture in the following year. During the depression years of the 1930s, she worked with the Works Progress Administration, Historic American Buildings Survey, and on the Century of Progress International Exhibition, held in Chicago in 1933–34. During her career she worked independently for various architects, was a designer for the Montgomery Ward chain of retail stores and architect of the Lindberg Engineering Company building, Chicago. Crawford died in 1988 in Springfield, Illinois.

23 Virgilio Marchi (1895–1960)

Design for a tram station and depot, *c.*1929

Perspective
Inscribed: *Stazione e deposito*
Signed: *V Marchi*
Pen, crayon & gouache on tracing paper (approx. 270 x 540)
Lit.: V. Marchi, *Italia nuova, architecttura nuova*. Roma: Franco Campitelli, 1931, reprd p.218, fig.46; Enrico Crispolti, *Attraverso l'architettura futurista*. Modena: Galleria Fonte d'Abisso, 1984, reprd p.199, fig.41

The influence of the Italian Futurist architect Antonio Sant'Elia upon Virgilio Marchi was profound, although it is unclear if the two men ever met. Sant'Elia died in 1916, the year that Marchi met F.T. Marinetti, the founder, in 1909, of the Futurist movement. Marchi was to become one of Sant'Elia's leading followers, spinning out ideas in the second Futurist wave during the 1920s and

23

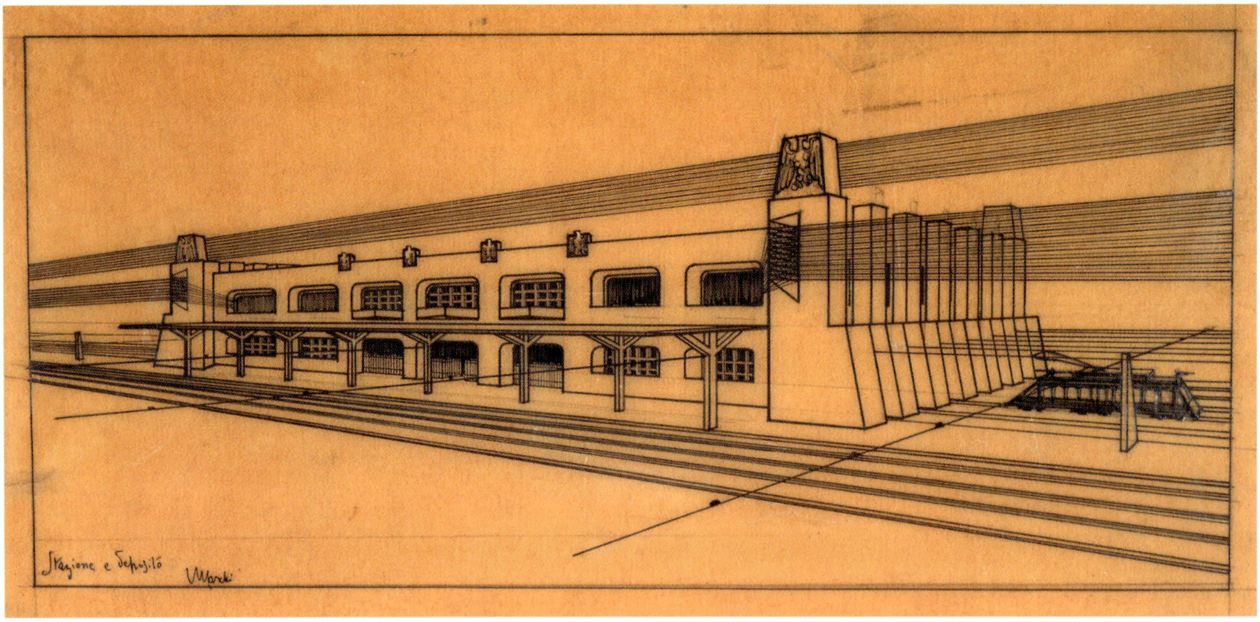

'30s when the movement grew to encompass almost all the arts.

In 1924, although written in 1919, Marchi published *Architecttura futurista* in homage to Sant'Elia, a manifesto expounding a break with historical traditions in order to establish a new way of living based on modern machinery, speed and movement. Marchi's work included visionary building designs that looked liked melting sculptures.

This drawing, however, for a tram station and depot, was published in 1931 in Marchi's second book *Italia nuova architecttura nuova*, 'New Italy, new architecture,' a very practical little presentation with a detailed section for a comprehensive system of tram lines throughout Rome, where Marchi lived. The monumentality of Sant'Elia's early images can been seen in the pylons guarding the openings of the tram station. The building is dominated by the long black streaks of tram and power lines, emphasising the dynamic and electrical forces so beloved of Futurists. The only decoration is the small sculpted eagles on the tops of the outer pylons, a nod to the Fascist regime in control of Italy.

In Naples during 1929, Marchi had created his own one-man show on Futurist architecture and 'scenotechnique', a combination natural to Marchi who made his principal contribution to Futurism in early cinema and theatre set design. This highly finished drawing may well have been shown at that exhibition.

24 Erik Gunnar Asplund (1885–1940) & Nils Einar Eriksson (1899–1978)

Design for the Music Pavilion, Stockholm Exhibition 1930, Sweden, *c.*1929

Perspective
Inscribed: *Musikestrad*
Pencil & black, red & green coloured pencil on tracing paper (272 x 380)
Lit.: Eva Rudberg, *The Stockholm Exhibition 1930: Modernism's breakthrough in Swedish architecture*. Stockholm: Stockholmia, 1999, reprd p.62

The exhibition held in Stockholm in 1930 was decisive in bringing Sweden to international notice as a country fluent, and now influential, in the new modernism of design and architecture. The unflagging principal architect behind the exhibition was Erik Gunnar Asplund, already well-known for such beautiful buildings as the neo-classical yet modern Stockholm Public Library, which had opened in 1928.

Asplund's chief assistant on the exhibition was Nils Einar Eriksson, who collaborated with Asplund on the site's most famous building, the glass and steel Paradise Restaurant. The Music Pavilion, however, was Eriksson's design, carried out in Asplund's office.

The structure is a band shell: a simple thin curving metal shell, with pipe columns and an interior clad with birchwood plywood which a contemporary commentator observed, was 'treated to look like a polished Stradivarius'. A lyre crowns the top right corner.

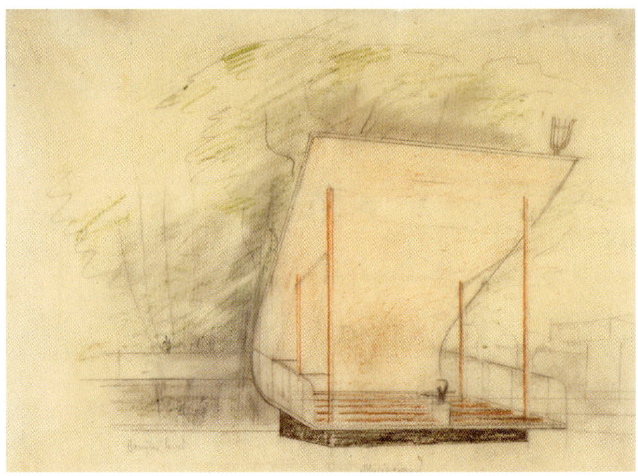

24

25 Erik Gunnar Asplund (1885–1940)

Design for judges' and court officials' chair, Law Courts Annex, Gothenburg, Sweden, *c.*1937

Sketch plan, side elevations & details
Pencil on paper (approx. 220 x 350)
Lit.: Filippo Alison, *Erik Gunnar Asplund: mobili e oggetti*. Milano: Electa, 1985, pp.104–105; Stuart Wrede, *The architecture of Erik Gunnar Asplund*. Cambridge, Mass.: MIT Press, 1980

25

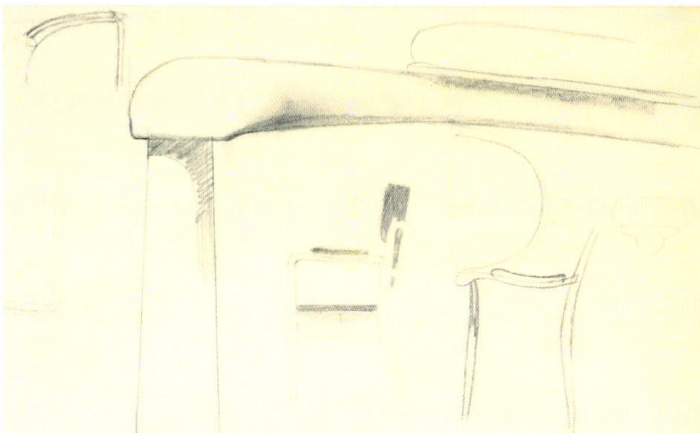

Asplund designed all the furniture for the extension he had added to the Gothenburg Law Courts building in the late 1930s. This annex, which is considered a major work in Asplund's *oeuvre*, presented a stark and austere façade right next to the classical pile of the original. But Asplund's interior was rich and modern in that Scandinavian Modernism of warm wooden walls and large open spaces.

This drawing is for the chairs to be used by judges and court officials in the several courtrooms. The design went through many stages, tending towards a high back to denote authority. In the end, however, the back was lowered but the profile of a wide top and pinched base retained. As in the side elevation in this drawing, seat and arms were covered in leather, as was the back which also had studs.

This design is almost as executed, except for the vertical and horizontal joint of the arm, which Asplund is exploring in the large detail which cuts across this drawing. As executed, the joint was continuous, retaining the line of the bentwood. In the judges' chair, this joint takes a gentle curve, whereas in the court officials' near-identical chair, the joint is closer to ninety degrees.

The design of this chair is considered of great importance as a precursor of post-Second World War Danish furniture (Wrede, p.171).

26 Le Corbusier, born Charles Édouard Jeanneret (1887–1965)

Design for additions to La Petite Maison, Corscaux, Switzerland, 1930

Sketch plan & perspective
Inscribed: *dalles / chez Carme / acheter / pour / l'atelier* [ie. buy stone slabs for the studio at Carme] */ maison du lac / á equipper d'l mur de 6 m avec atelier pour mo..st..y* [illegible] *de 6m* [ie. lake house to be equipped with a 6 meter wall with a studio for [?] 6 meters]
Signed & dated: (in architect's own hand) *Extrait / l'album Corb / de 1930* [ie. extracted from Le Corbusier's 1930 album]
Pen on sketchbook letter paper imprinted *Le Corbusier* (208 x 255)
Lit.: Le Corbusier, *Une Petite Maison, 1923*. Zurich: Editions Girsberger, 1954; W. Boesiger and H. Girsberger, *Le Corbusier, 1910–1965*. Zurich: Editions d'Architecture, 1986, pp.38-41; Deborah Gans, *The Le Corbusier Guide*. Princeton & London: Architectural Press, 2000, pp.158–161

Le Corbusier built La Petite Maison, also known as Maison du Lac, as a holiday home for his parents in 1923, just before his father died. It is situated on the edge of Lake Geneva, in a suburb of the resort town of Vevey. The architect often stayed here, with his mother and his brother Albert, a musician and composer. Madame Jeanneret celebrated her 90th birthday at the house, in 1950; she lived to be 101 years old.

In 1953, Le Corbusier designed and wrote a little commemorative book on La Petite Maison in which he called the house 'la machine à habiter', a machine for living in. Flat-roofed, with sliding walls and vanishing beds, this little villa was amongst Le Corbusier's earliest modernist experiments, before any of his celebrated buildings.

This sketch design dates from 1930 and illustrates Le Corbusier's ideas for making additions to the property. This was the year in which the local government decided to make the quiet road alongside the house into the major route between the west and the Simplon Pass, the fury of motor vehicles replacing, as he commented, 'le silence d'Arcadie'.

So here in the drawing is the little villa seen from the end of the garden terrace, with its covered porch held up by a pair of metal pipes and also with its famous 33 foot (11 metre) long single window, facing south over the lake. Replacing the hedge, Le Corbusier proposes the 6 metre high wall, the top line of which dominates this drawing, a barrier against the new noise. This was built, but had a stepped profile. The architect also suggests covering the lawn with square paving stones, which was not executed. However, his written suggestion on the drawing for a studio was carried out, and was erected at the end of the terrace behind the end wall, a quiet getaway where Albert wrote his music.

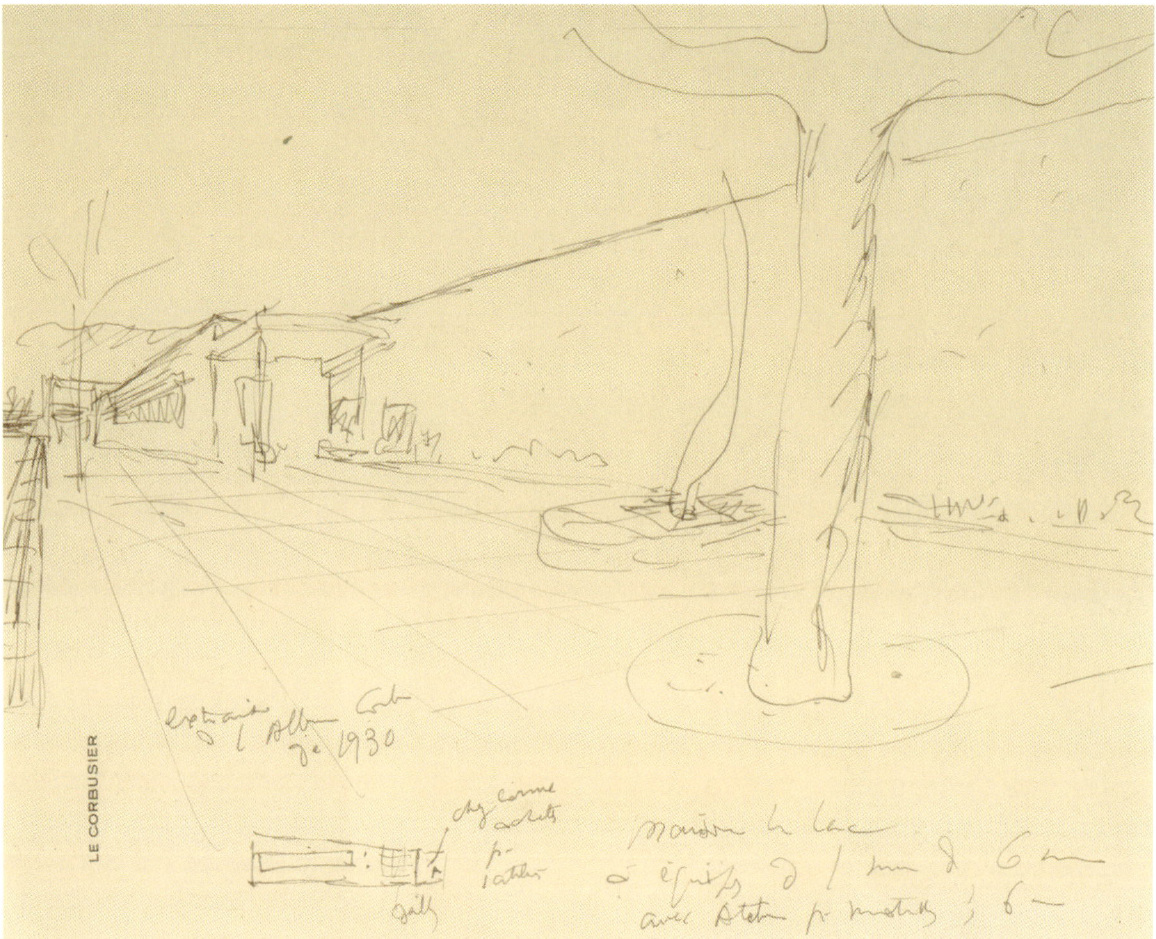

26

27 Richard Josef Neutra (1892–1970)

Competition design for the Griffith Observatory, Los Angeles, USA, *c.*1931

Aerial perspective
Inscribed: *LA Planetarium. Birdseye view*
Signed: *Richard J. Neutra Arch*
Pencil & coloured crayon on paper (approx. 375 x 260)

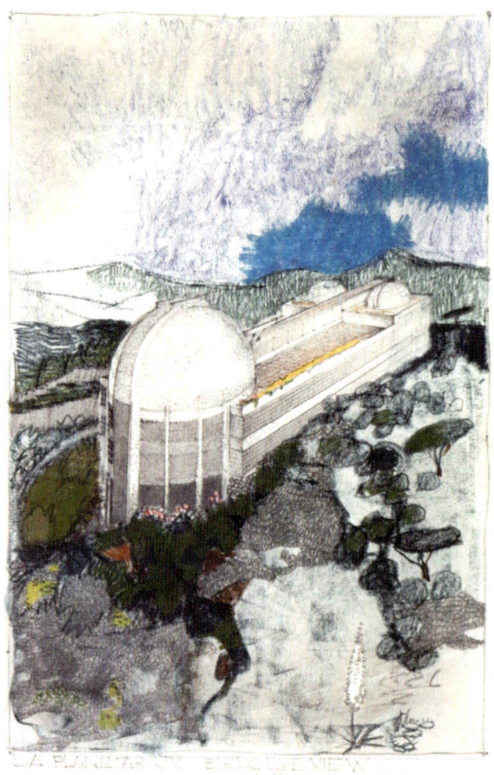

27

This is a master drawing by a master architect who enjoyed creating colourful and atmospheric perspectives. It is Neutra's entry for the 1931 competition for the Griffith Observatory, sited on the south slope of Mount Hollywood. Interestingly, Neutra had just completed in 1929 the building which many consider his classic, the large and modernist Lovell House, also in the Hollywood Hills.

The design consists of two domes: one large to contain the planetarium – a new innovation for the period – and one small for the observatory, to house the great 12-inch Zeiss telescope. The pair are joined by the long body of the building in a silhouette which loosely echoes Erich Mendelsohn's Einstein Tower, Potsdam.

Neutra did not win the competition, and the Griffith Observatory was instead built to the more traditionally formal Beaux Arts design of John C. Austin working with Frederick M. Ashley.

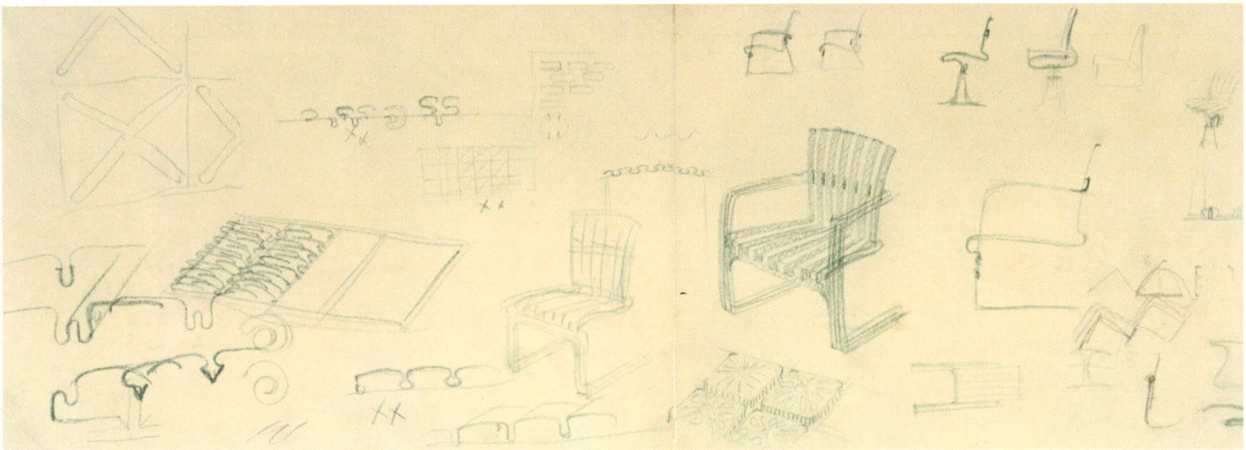

28

28 Ludwig Mies van der Rohe (1886–1969)

Studies for chairs, *c.*1933–34

Pencil & green crayon on tracing paper (approx. 200 x 580)
Lit.: Ludwig Glaeser, *Ludwig Mies van der Rohe: furniture and furniture drawings from the Design Collection and the Mies van der Rohe Archive, the Museum of Modern Art, New York*. New York: Museum of Modern Art, 1977, reprd p.15

In the late 1920s and early 1930s, part of this time while director of the Bauhaus school, the architect Mies van der Rohe designed several classic pieces of furniture, many of them still in production today. His first works were cantilevered, made from the swooping curves of bent tubular metal frames. But perhaps his most well-known work, seen starkly grouped in many a modern office building entrance foyer, is the Barcelona chair, made of comfortable leather upholstery set upon a criss-cross steel frame, originally created for the Mies-designed German Pavilion at the 1929 World Exposition in Barcelona, Spain.

In the years between the closing of the Bauhaus by the Nazis in 1933, and Mies's emigration to the United States in 1937, he found time to return to furniture design. This drawing dates from this period, around 1933–34, when he made several hundred similar sketches. It is a long sheet, sprinkled with different ideas for chairs, mainly cantilevered, and with details for their construction. The largest images in the centre of the drawing are for a chair with bentwood slatted seat and back. The frame could be either metal or wood. In 1935, Mies applied for a German patent for twelve different runners, one of which bears a striking similarity to this frame. The details appear to be for different types of fabric and leather weaves, cushioning and joints.

None of the furniture designs from this period went into production.

29 Ludwig Mies van der Rohe (1886–1969)

Preliminary design for Mountain House, possibly Merano, Italy, *c.*1934

Aerial view
Pencil on paper mounted on card (210 x 298)
Lit.: Terence Riley and Barry Bergdoll, *Mies in Berlin*. New York: Museum of Modern Art, 2001, pp.280–83

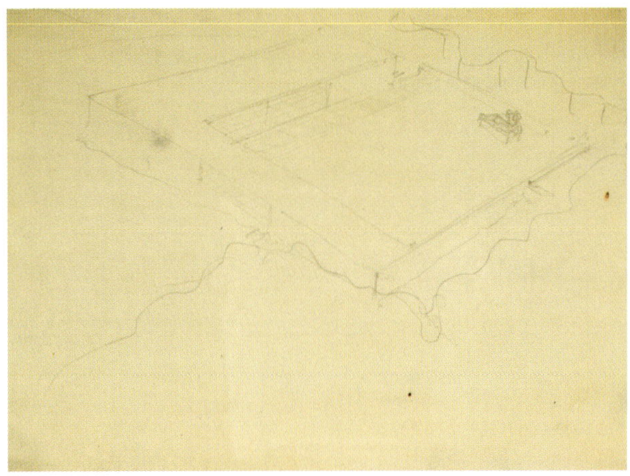

29

As director of the Bauhaus in Berlin, Mies van der Rohe was forced to close the school by pressure from the Nazis. He thereupon moved to Lugano in Switzerland with his partner and a few students. This drawing for a house dates from this Swiss period. In earlier days, he had spent holidays with his family in Merano, in the South Tyrolean Alps; this house design, judging by the enclosing jagged line probably indicating a rocky site, might be for a location in this mountain setting. It was never built.

The flat-roofed house is L-shape in plan, with a large glass window running the inside on to the large courtyard, and another window or opening under a covered way, facing out. A sculpture graces the courtyard.

In 1947, the Museum of Modern Art in New York, which incidentally has several other drawings for this project in its Mies collection, held a retrospective of the architect's work. This design, it is said, was seen by and influenced other such Modern architects as Charles Eames and Philip Johnson.

30 Paul Philippe Cret (1876–1945)

Design for a monumental building, *c.*1935

Elevation
Pencil & black, green & brown crayon on tracing paper (285 x 425)
Lit.: Paul Philippe Cret Collection, The Architectural Archives of the University of Pennsylvania and the Athenaeum of Philadelphia. On-line at www.philadelphiabuildings.org/pab/index.cfm

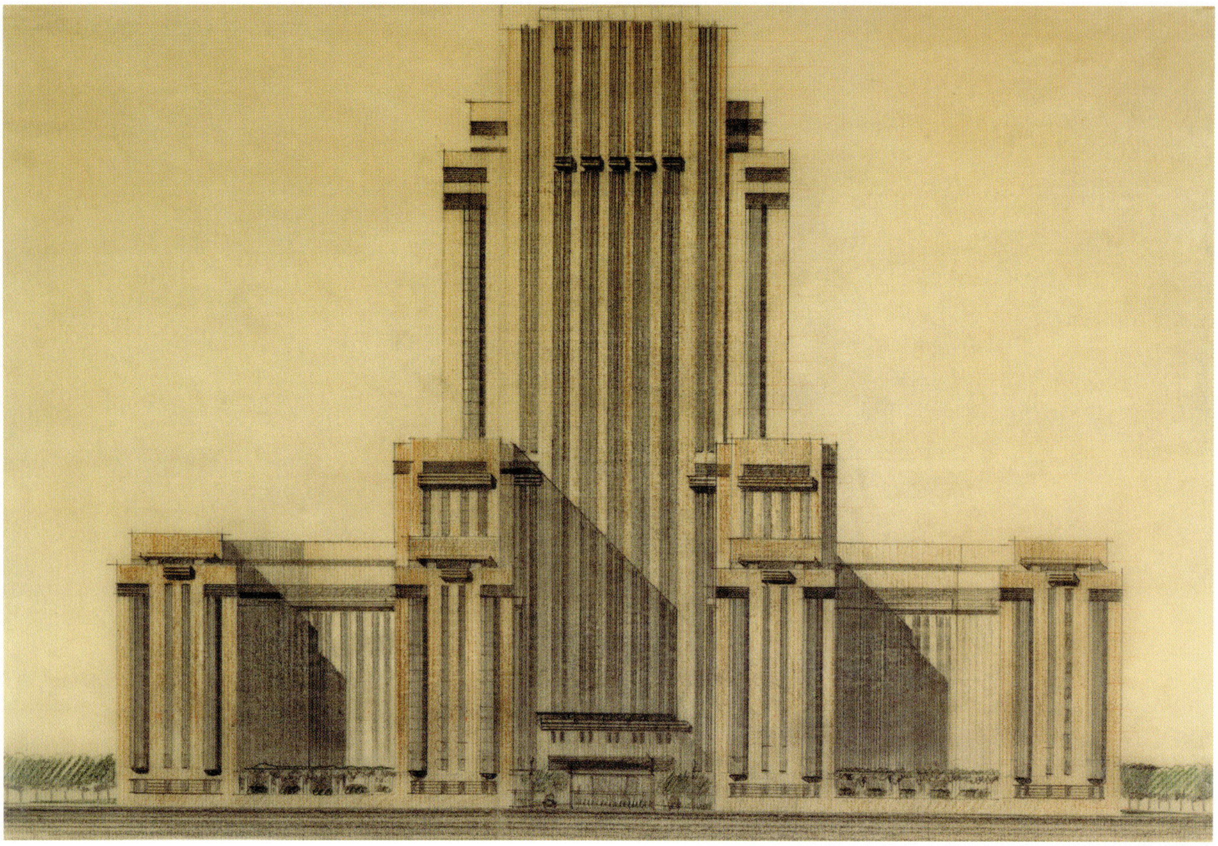 30

French-born and having studied architecture at the Ecole des Beaux-Arts in Paris, Paul Cret had the ideal education for Beaux Arts-loving America. By 1903, he had been recruited to teach in Philadelphia, at the University of Pennsylvania, where he remained (except for five years with the French army during World War I) until his death. In his lifetime, he nurtured many talented pupils including Louis Kahn, built up a thriving practice, and gained a national reputation as an architect of large commercial and civic buildings, bridges and memorials.

This design for an unidentified building is typical of the monumental buidings created by Cret in the mid- to late 1930s, works like the Greenberg Parkway Apartments in Philadelphia and the US Naval Medical Center in Bethesda, Maryland where the entrance lies at the base of a giant tower, hemmed in by powerful wings. As a pencil drawing, it is a tour de force of the hard-edge assurance of a modern architect still working within the classical idiom.

31 William Lescaze (1896–1969)

Design for the Garret A. Hobart III house and studio, Tuxedo Park, New York, USA, 1938

Aerial perspective
Signed & dated: *Lescaze arct / Jan 30–38*
Blueprint with pencil & coloured chalk added (310 x 495)
Lit.: Lorraine Willing Lanmon, *William Lescaze, Architect*. Cranbury, New Jersey: Associated University Press, 1987, p.113; *Architects' drawings from the collection of Barbara Pine.* Evanston, Illinois: Mary and Leigh Block Gallery, Northwestern University, 1987, reprd p.29 (incorrect identification)

William Lescaze built two houses in Tuxedo Park, that town just north-west of New York City so exclusive that it has a formal men's suit named after it. The nearby Alfred Loomis house, completed only a few years earlier, had been a successful experiment for a client who was a patron of scientific research. That house had been modern movement, similar in style to this design for the Garret A. Hobart III house, but with the emphasis on strict controls over temperature, humidity and sound insulation.

Using a blueprint is an interesting and rare mannerism in architectural presentation designs, as it was a method of reproducing drawings normally reserved for working drawings. Lescaze hand-coloured this blueprint to make it a showpiece gift for the client who, appropriately, was an artist and sculptor. In fact, Hobart's studio can be seen clearly on the drawing, with its sloping glass skylight to the right of the entrance.

The house sits on the edge of a lake, seen in the background of the drawing behind the trees. The large terrace laid out in herringbone brickwork (rendered in pink cross-hatching) affords views over the lake and also, retained from the earlier house on the site, the formal gardens below approached by the elaborate descending stairs.

The Swiss-born architect William Lescaze, who had moved to America in 1920, is credited for giving New York City its first International style building of its kind, his own house on East 48th Street, with a façade of glass bricks, dating from 1934. England can also boast an assembly of Lescaze early modern movement houses designed in the 1930s for Dartington School in Devon.

31

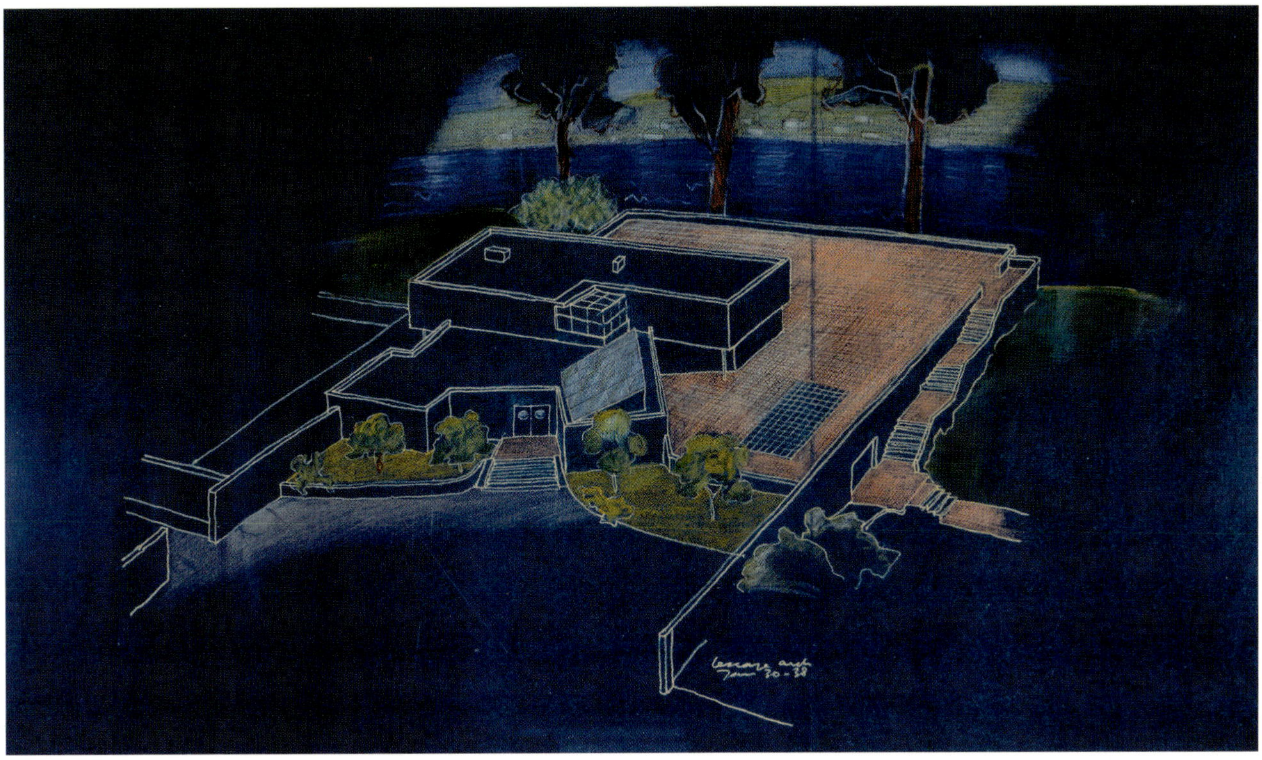

32 Frank Lloyd Wright (1867–1959)

Design for Research Tower, Johnson Wax, Racine, Wisconsin, USA, *c.*1944

Perspective
Signed: *Frank Lloyd Wright* & (blind stamp) *Frank Lloyd Wright Foundation*
Pen, pencil, gouache & coloured washes on paper (355 x 930)
Lit.: *Architects' drawings from the collection of Barbara Pine*. Evanston, Illinois: Mary and Leigh Block Gallery, Northwestern University, 1987, p.47, reprd p.12; Brian Carter, *Johnson Wax administration building and research tower*. London: Phaidon, 1998

In 1939, Frank Lloyd Wright completed the Administration Building for S. C. Johnson and Son, more commonly known as Johnson Wax after the company's most popular product. A few years later, he was asked back to add a tower for research laboratories.

The low structure of the administration block, seen clearly here in the drawing, has one of Wright's most famous interiors, with its mushroom-shaped columns. This drawing dates from the early stages of the design for the tower, around 1944, with seven white bands of glazing set between the pink of the Cherokee Red brick. When completed in 1949, however, the research tower had been reduced to six bands. The glazing was extremely novel: stacks of wide Pyrex tubes – 'test tubes' they were jokingly called.

The drawing itself is very typical of the presentation perspectives from the FLW office of the period, with the image restrained within a broken or partial border outline and the architect's initials or signature in a red box. The image is long, low and horizontal like the houses which Frank Lloyd Wright designed in the 'Prairie style'.

32

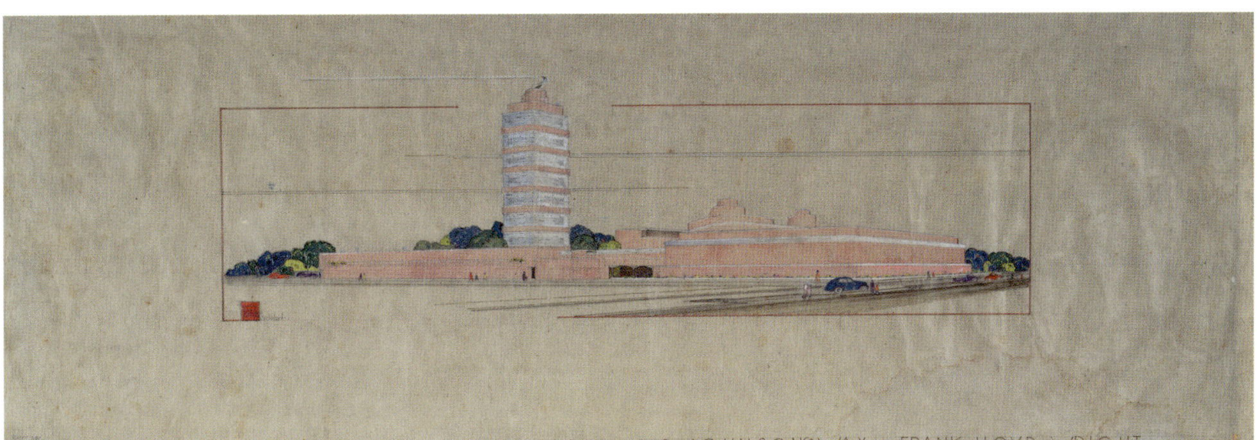

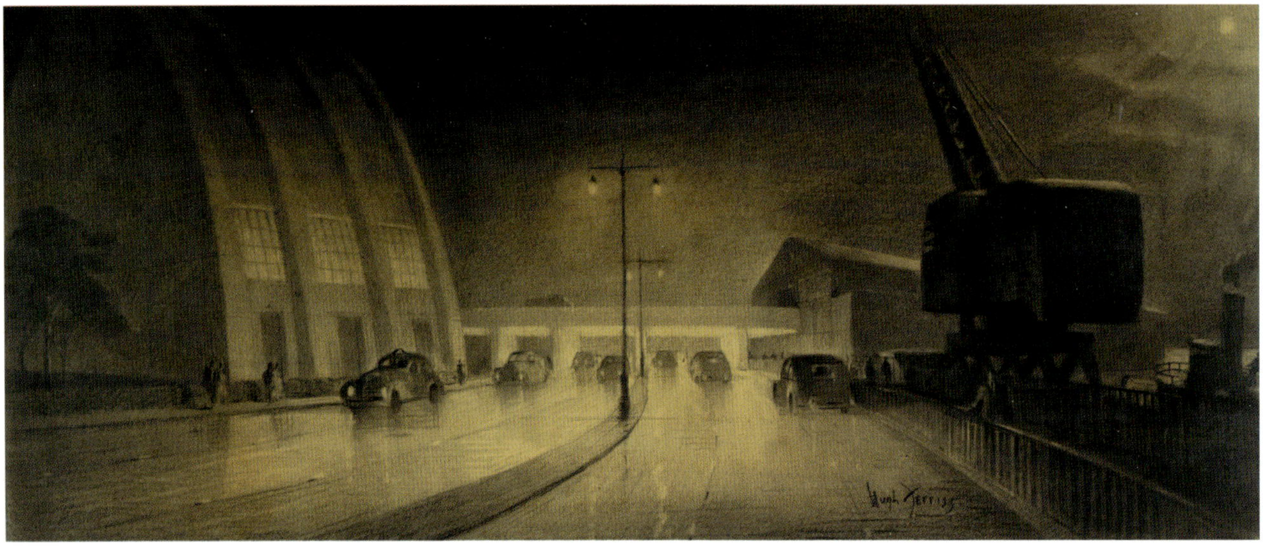

33

33 Hugh Ferriss (1889–1962)

View of the Municipal Asphalt Plant, New York, USA, *c.*1945

Exterior view
Signed: *Hugh Ferriss*
Charcoal on paper (285 x 560)
Lit.: *Architects' drawings from the collection of Barbara Pine.* Evanston, Illinois: Mary and Leigh Block Gallery, Northwestern University, 1987, reprd p.18

Hugh Ferriss is considered the master of all architectural artists in twentieth-century America, and this is a fine and typical example, tonally executed in the black and white of his favoured charcoal. It is also a night view, another Ferriss preference, creating an atmosphere evocative of an Edward Hopper painting.

The Municipal Asphalt Plant is a New York landmark. Ferriss drew it just after its completion in 1944, with the rush of traffic on East River Drive and a crane and warehouse edging the Hudson River figuring as prominently as the curving form of the plant building, which is only partially shown. There is even the ghostly silhouette of a tugboat coming into dock.

The Municipal Asphalt Plant, with its rows of glass block windows, is reputed to be the first successful concrete parabolic arch building in the United States. The architects were Ely Jacques Kahn, who had a reputation as a fine Art Deco skyscraper architect, and his partner Robert Allen Jacobs, who had briefly studied with Le Corbusier in Paris. In 1982, the building was converted to its present use as the Asphalt Green Sports and Arts Center.

34 Gio Ponti (1891–1979)

Design for a display cabinet made for No. 7 via della Spiga, Milan, Italy, 1946

Plans & elevations
Inscribed: *MO 48 / a della Spiga 7 / 10 / tavolo / ufficio* [ie. office desk] / *qui* [ie. here] / *da fare per / ottobre* [ie. to be made by October] / *civate*
Signed & dated: *G.P. / 11 / 8 / 46*
Pencil, black & brown pen & green crayon on two-hole binder paper (286 x 228)

Gio Ponti is a towering figure in twentieth-century Italian architecture and design: inspired creator of ceramics, glass and tableware; founder and editor of *Domus* magazine from 1928 to 1979; architect of such celebrated buildings as the Pirelli tower in Milan, and designer of interiors and furniture pieces such as this exquisitely beautiful display cabinet.

Standing on long tapering legs, the cabinet is crowned by a pair of urns and stylistically follows in the neo-classical modernism that Ponti often favoured from the 1920s until the late 1940s. In the centre is a niche containing a show piece, probably a ceramic figure, which remains in view even when the doors are closed. It also seems, judging from the plan on the lower right, that this recess is illuminated from the back; or perhaps when the doors are opened the light is tripped. With the doors swung back,

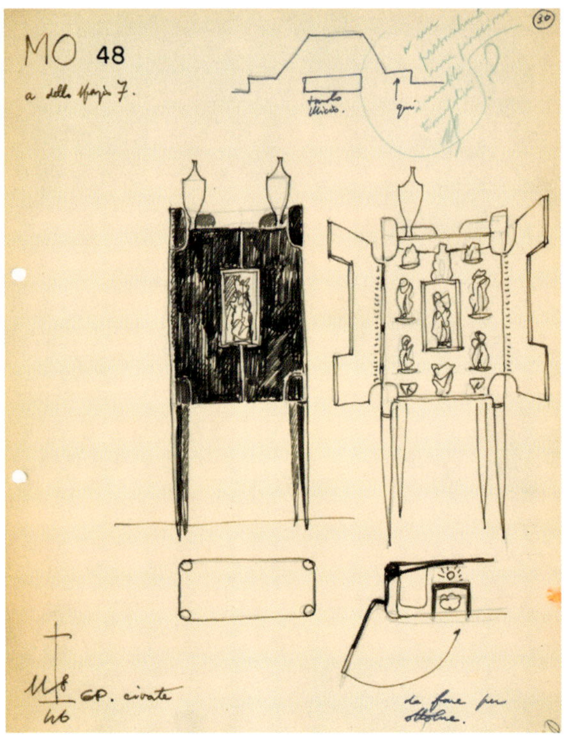

34

a series of little shelves is revealed, for more objects, set on a curving backdrop.

By good fortune, Barbara Pine purchased from another source an accompanying drawing by Ponti to this design, for a bedroom in an apartment on Via della Spiga, in the fashionable section of Milan. The display cabinet was to fit in an alcove, as shown in the plan at the top of this drawing, prominently facing the owner's bed.

In the bottom left of this drawing, to the right of the stylized date and initials at the base of a stylized cross (the design which he had used in some of the chapels that he had built), Ponti has signed 'civate', which was the name of his small house in Brianza to which he and his family had moved during the Second World War.

35 Frederick Kiesler (1890–1965)

Sketch designs for an 'endless' piece of furniture, 1947

Plan, perspectives & details
Inscribed: *Chair - Table - Bench* & materials & techniques noted
Signed & dated: *Kiesler* / [illegible] / *47*
Pen on paper (500 x 358)
Lit.: Dieter Bogner and Peter Noever, eds, *Frederick J. Kiesler: endless space*. Ostfildern-Ruit: Hatje Cantz, 2001; *Architects' drawings from the collection of Barbara Pine.* Evanston, Illinois: Mary and Leigh Block Gallery, Northwestern University, 1987, reprd p.47

After studying art and architecture in his native Vienna, Kiesler moved flawlessly from one famous early twentieth-century artistic movement to the next. He was a member of the De Stijl group, directed the Austrian section of the famous 1925 Art Deco Exposition in Paris, and moved in 1926 to New York to become a prominent designer of American Modernism, especially in stage set design. In 1947, the year of this drawing, Kiesler installed the last important Surrealist exhibition at the Galerie Maeght in Paris. His masterpiece, created with his pupil Armand Bartos, is the Shrine of the Book (1959–1965), a circular sanctuary in Jerusalem built to house the Dead Sea Scrolls.

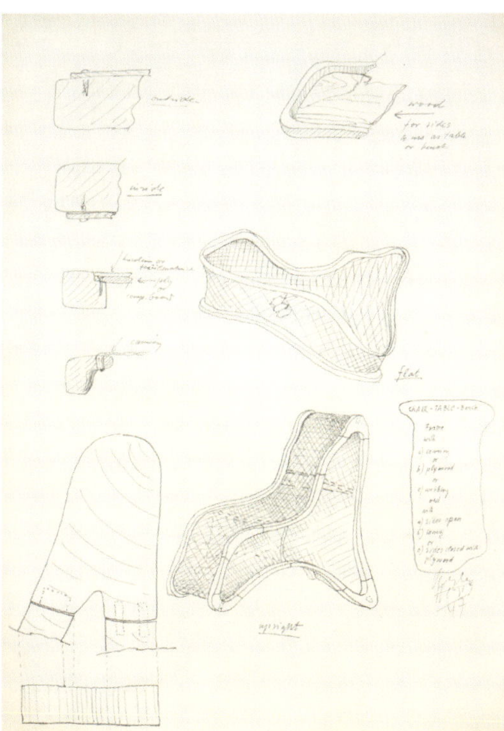

35

The spatial concept of 'endlessness' informed almost all aspects of Kiesler's work: he designed the Endless House, which although never built was extremely influential on generations of architects, as was his Endless Theatre. The design in this drawing is for a piece of furniture which too is 'endless'; an object that can be turned on any of its sides – multi-functional, kinetic and bio-morphic. 'Chair – Table – Bench', Kiesler suggests by his inscription and to be made of interchangeable and various materials: caneing, plywood, webbing. Endlessness, for Kiesler, meant a continuous flow between man, object and the environment.

This design does not seem to have gone into production and was based upon the chairs, benches and display stands which Kiesler had designed and installed in 1942 in Peggy Guggenheim's Art of the Century Gallery in New York.

36 Paolo Soleri (born 1919)

Design for house, known as Arizonian Nest, 1948

Section & aerial perspective
Scale: 1/8th inch to 1 foot
Inscribed: *Section and Front*
Signed & dated: *Paolo Soleri 1948*
Pencil, colour pen & coloured washes on paper (370 x 600)
Lit.: Antonietta Iolanda, *Soleri: architecture as human ecology*. New York: Monacelli, 2003, reprd p.107; *Architects' drawings from the collection of Barbara Pine.* Evanston, Illinois: Mary and Leigh Block Gallery, Northwestern University, 1987, p.41, reprd p.40

The visionary architect Paolo Soleri lives and works in the utopian desert community of Arconsanti, Arizona, which he began to create in 1970. It is his model 'archology', a harmonious marriage of architecture and ecology. The buildings are mainly concrete, organic in form, and very environment friendly. Funding is by the sale of windbells.

Upon graduating in 1946 with his degree in architecture from the university in his native Turin, Italy, Soleri won a scholarship as an apprentice to Frank Lloyd Wright at Taliesin West, Wright's own Arizona desert office community. This drawing dates from this period, or probably a few months after Soleri left at the end of 1948. The design responds to at least two of FLW's famous schemes: the projecting overhang of Fallingwater and the cone-shape of the Solomon Guggenheim Museum.

Like a natural outgrowth from a mountain's edge, this flying saucer of a house nestles into the rocks. The roof dome is composed of two layers: an opaque section which rotates on top of a translucent section. These glide around each other, worked by a timed motor, keeping segments of the house shaded from the scorching desert sun. Apparently, judging by the section, the roof also pulls back.

Although the Arizonian Nest house was not built, in the following year Soleri and his friend Mark Mills did construct a desert home for Soleri's mother-in-law which incorporated a glass and aluminium dome.

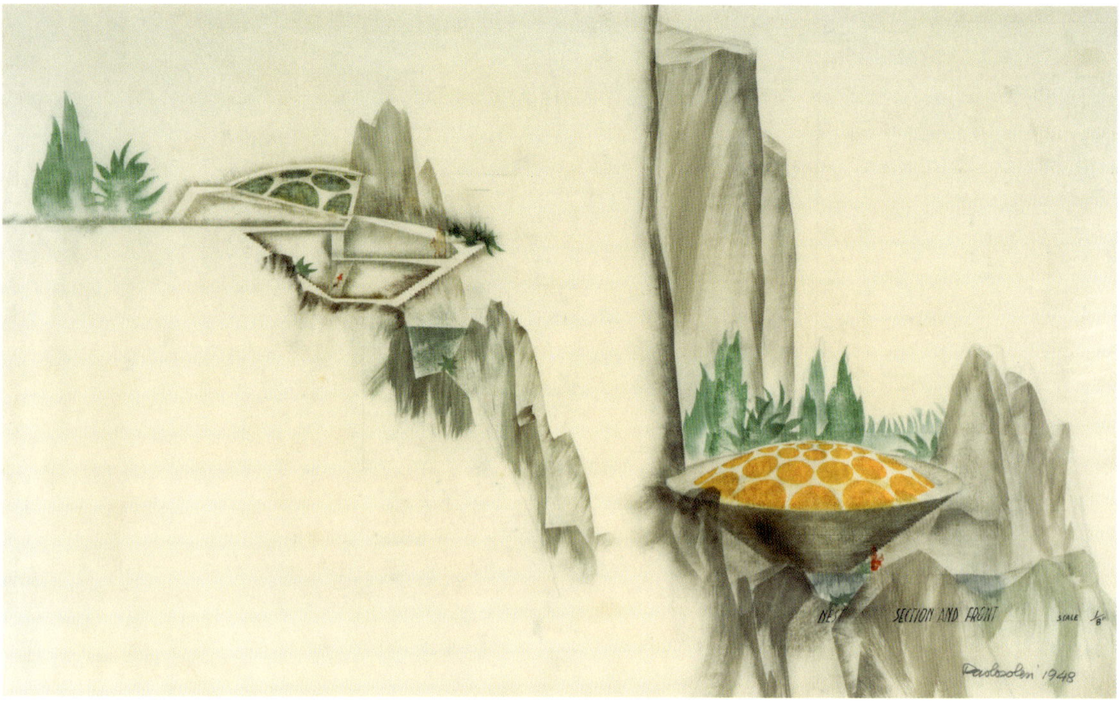

36

37 Álvaro Siza (born 1933)

Sketch design for the Boa Nova Tea House, Leça da Palmeira, Portugal, *c.*1960

Sketch plans and perspectives
Signed: *Siza*
Pen on 2-ring binder paper (268 x 202, top left edge torn)
Lit.: Álvaro Siza, *Boa Nova Tea House*. Lisboa: Blau, 1999; Kenneth Frampton, *Álvaro Siza: complete works*. London: Phaidon, 2000, pp.82–89

Álvaro Siza is Portugal's most celebrated architect. And this drawing is for his most well-known, and one of his earliest buildings, the Boa Nova Tea House. In the top sketch of this sheet, the blocked form of the chimney rises over the lower forms of the tea house's roof, the scratched surfaces representing the rocky outcrop where the building stands at the edge of the Atlantic Ocean.

The architecture and siting of the tea house is sensitively handled, adapted to the contours of the topography. The swooping rooflines, with deep eaves, echo the crashing waves. The car park is located at a little distance from the building, and the approach is by a winding path, emphasised by Siza in this drawing by the zigzag lines in both the little sketches and plan. It is an oft repeated observation that this route is the visitor's Calvary, the Stations of the Cross missing from the chapel located next to the tea house.

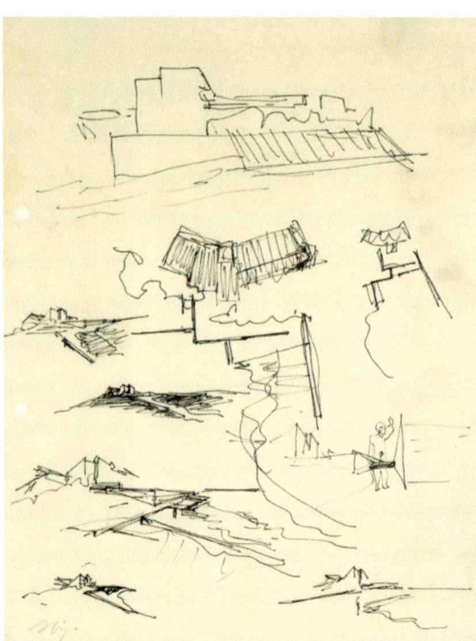

37

38 Álvaro Siza (born 1933)

Studies for drawing board and stool for the Carlo Ramos Pavilion, Faculty of Architecture, Porto, Portugal, *c.*1985

Inscribed: *Lino* [ie. linoleum, or linen, or a name] / *desenhar* [ie. drawing] / *mesas* [ie. tables] / *escrivaninhas* [ie. work desk] / *bencor* [ie. stool] & components and materials given *executar* [ie. to be made] such as *persa* [ie. legs]
Pen on paper (295 x 205)
Lit.: Luiz Trigueiros, *Álvaro Siza 1954–1976*. Lisbon: Blau, 1997, p.286 (photograph of drawing board and stool as executed)

In the mid-1980s, the Portuguese architect Álvaro Siza designed a small studio building as an addition to the Faculty of Architecture in Porto (Oporto in Portugese), where the architect teaches and practices. This drawing is a flurry of ideas for a drawing board and accompanying stool to be used by the students. The variant stool designs are based on tripodal legs and a rotating seat which raises and lowers its height.

The table and stool as executed were much simpler, with straightforward frames made of tubular steel. The stool, however, was designed cleverly with the four tall legs not touching the ground but rather floating upon a rectangle of tubing which had an elevated bar for a foot rest.

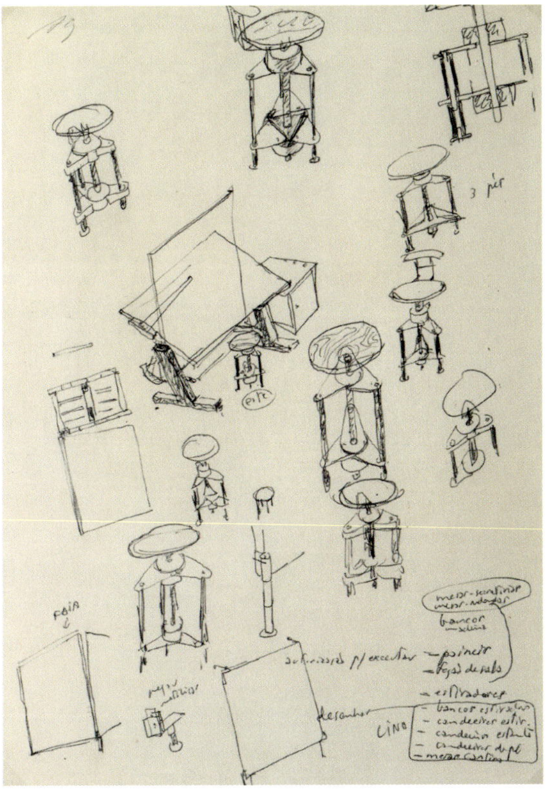

38

39 Louis I. Kahn (1901–1974)

Design for the Inner Court, Indian Institute of Management, Ahmedabad, India, 1963

Perspective with additional sketch plans, elevations, perspectives & details
Inscribed: *Coloured pencil sketch*
Signed & dated: *Kahn / May 1963*
Pen & coloured pencil on yellow tracing paper (585 x 640)
Lit.: *The Louis I. Kahn archive: personal drawings: the completely illustrated catalogue of the drawings in the Louis I. Kahn Collection, University of Pennsylvania and Pennsylvania Historical and Museum Commission*. New York & London: Garland, 1987; Joseph Rykwert, *Louis Kahn*. New York: Abrams, 2001, pp.154–73

Louis Kahn is the highly respected and influential Modern Movement architect renowned for his bold and simple compositions, both in plan and structure, and his use of brick and concrete in monumental massing. All these qualities are evident in this extremely fine drawing, made in the early stages of one of Kahn's most important works – a managerial institute in India which was to include a library, dormitories and study centres.

The principal perspective in this drawing is a view looking along the Inner Court. The enormous rectangular forms of the buildings are in place, somewhat similar to Kahn's well-known assemblage of concrete laboratory buildings for the Jonas Salk Institute in California, completed a few years earlier, which also

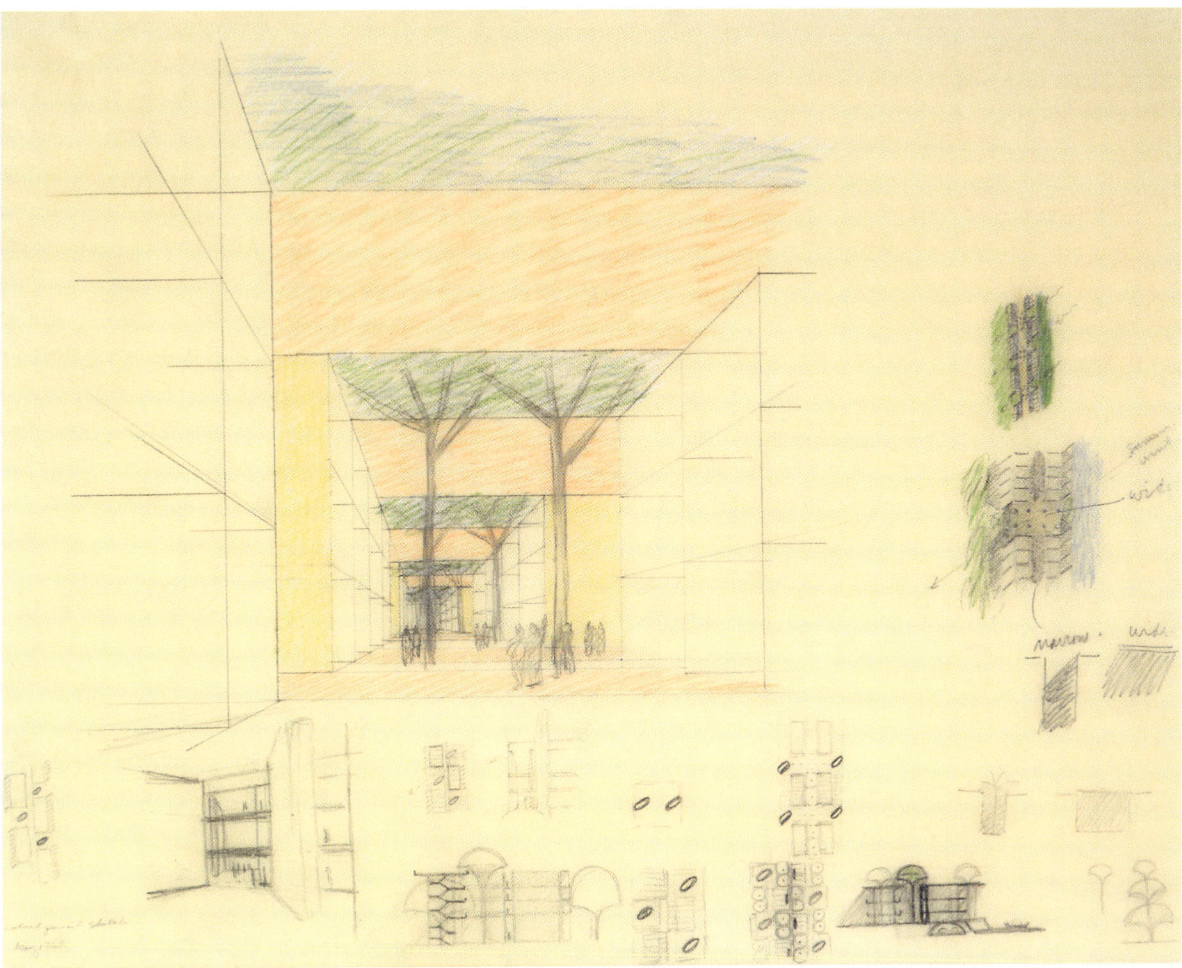

39

bordered a long court. A small perspective in the lower left gives a better idea of the monumentality of the architecture.

Kahn evokes traditional Indian precedents with ventilation and shading from the heat of the hot sun by stretching large canopies of cloth overhead, which in this drawing are coloured orange. At regular intervals between these, he plants towering trees, their green bowers made to fit the geometry. In the small elevation, the stylistic tree tops are clearly visible. And, playfully, in the lower right, Kahn experiments with different tree shapes. The architect's Beaux Arts training comes to the fore in the sharp regularity of the little sketch plans.

Even though, as built, the cloth canopies and trees were not used, cooling was achieved beautifully by the Inner Court and the massive red brick walls, arches, pierced openings, verandas and light wells throughout the complex.

40 Richard Meier (born 1934)

Design for the Hoffman House, East Hampton, New York, 1967

Axonometric perspective
Signed & dated: *Richard Meier 1967* & (rubber stamp) *Richard Meier Architect / 56 East 53 Street, New York*
Pencil on tracing paper (595 x 670)
Lit.: *Architects' drawings from the collection of Barbara Pine.* Evanston, Illinois: Mary and Leigh Block Gallery, Northwestern University, 1987, reprd p.30

This drawing, with its exacting lines, is an axonometric projection, an appropriate method to show off the angles of the Hoffman House which is an abstracted interlocking of double squares and geometric forms. Designed and built in 1966–67, this was only Richard Meier's second completed building. Today, Meier is one of America's most well-known architects, designer of such respected works as the Getty Center in Los Angeles.

The view here is towards the rear of the house, with emphasis given to the pierced screen which cuts through the entrance and then screens a part of the elevation. A similar screen at the front of the house is not shown in this drawing, nor are the differing heights of the roof. But the tall, free-standing chimney for the living room is clearly detailed, a feature which allowed a window quirkily to be placed directly over the fireplace.

41 Richard Meier (born 1934)

Design for an armchair, *c.*1979

Plans, elevations & axonometric perspectives
Signed: *Richard Meier*
Pencil, pen, wash & white gouache on paper (440 x 660)
Lit.: *Domus*, No. 636, February 1983, p.64; Mark Emery, *Furniture by architects: international masterpieces of twentieth-century design and where to buy them.* New York: Abrams, 1988, pp.178, 204–07; *Architects' drawings from the collection of Barbara Pine.* Evanston, Illinois: Mary and Leigh Block Gallery, Northwestern University, 1987, reprd p.31

Richard Meier first designed this chair as part of the suite of light-finished oak furniture which he had created for the Aye Simon Reading Room in the Solomon R. Guggenheim Museum in New York in 1977–78. Meier maintains that a source of inspiration had been furniture designs of Frank Lloyd Wright, the building's architect, especially in the spacing of the horizontal back members. Also, at this time Meier was fascinated with the geometry of the square and cube, especially doubled (as witness the juxtaposed double square of the plan of the Hoffman House drawing – cat. 39) and these forms appear in this chair design. But, in overall appearance, the greatest debt goes to Josef Hoffmann's famous bentwood armchair from the beginning of the twentieth century.

This chair went into manufacture in the early 1980s by Knoll International, made of maple, left natural or finished in glossy black or white, as highlighted in this drawing.

42 Paul Rudolph (1918–1997)

Study for the Government Centre, New Haven, Connecticut, USA, *c.*1970

Elevation with details added
Inscribed: with calculations & measurements
Pencil & coloured pencil on tracing paper (450 x 1260, left edge torn)
Lit.: David Gebhard and Deborah Nevins, *200 years of American architectural drawing.* New York: Whitney Library of Design for the Architectural League of New York and the American Federation of Arts, 1977, pp.280–82, reprd pp.280–81; *Architects' drawings from the collection of Barbara Pine.* Evanston, Illinois: Mary and Leigh Block Gallery, Northwestern University, 1987, p.35

40

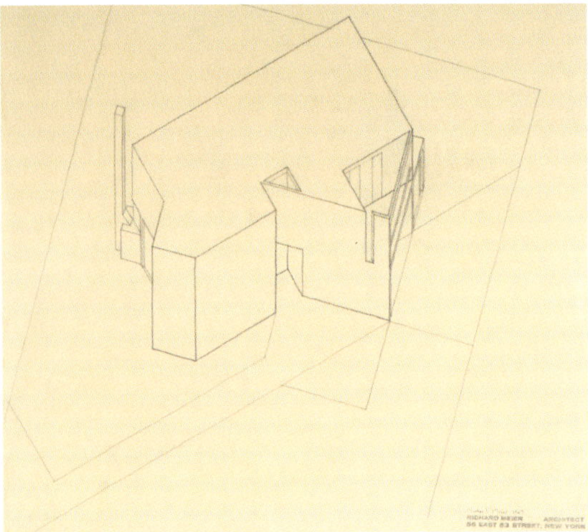

41

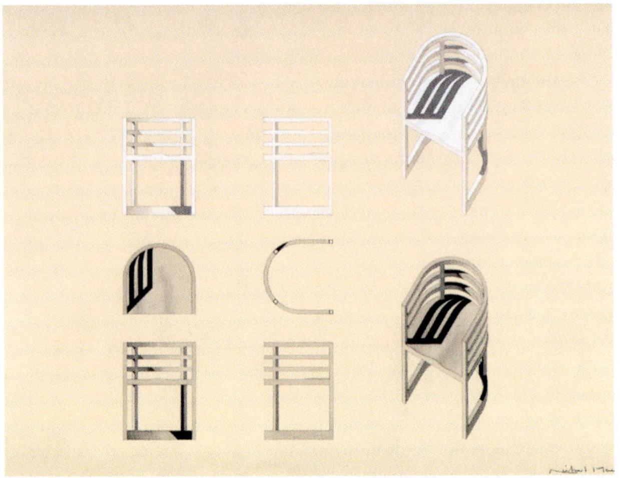

42

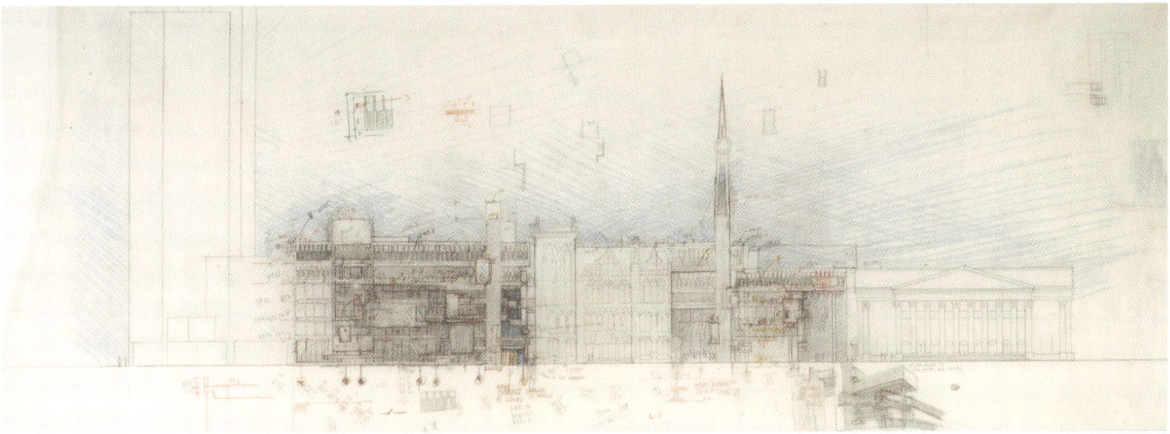

This is a large and intense drawing, with a raw finesse keeping in spirit with Paul Rudolph's own exposed concrete architecture. It presents the redevelopment of a row of local government buildings in the city of New Haven. Rudolph's two main interventions are the darker, more heavily worked areas of the sheet: on the left is the massive form of the library; to the right is the new city hall, with it minaret-like clock tower. Between is the pointed-arched outline of the old Victorian city hall, and at the extreme right, the silhouette of the existing neo-classical post office.

Paul Rudolph had created the Boston Government Center, between 1962 and 1971, a great Brutalist work which was both lauded and reviled with equal intensity. The young British architect Norman Foster, for example, was so impressed by Rudolph's architecture that he took his Master's degree under him at Yale University. Like this scheme for New Haven, Rudolph's designs made no concession in terms of style to their surroundings; the architect played on relating scale and proportion, in a hard Modernism, and always in unremitting concrete. These characteristics made Rudolph unfashionable by the late 1970s, and he received few commissions in America. However, he scored great success in later years designing the most wondrous high-rise buildings, great monolithic works of concrete architecture in fantastic shapes.

43 Robert Venturi (born 1925)

Design for alterations & additions to the Allen Memorial Art Museum, Oberlin College, Oberlin, Ohio, USA, *c.*1973

Sketch perspective
Signed & dated: *Michael Venturi '73*
Pen on yellow tracing paper (approx. 275 x 735)
Lit.: A. Sanmartin ed., *Venturi, Rauch & Scott Brown*. London: Academy Editions, 1986, pp.86–93

This drawing is about the essence of the design. In the minimum of strokes, Venturi compares and contrasts his extension (done in conjunction with his partner John Rauch) to the older existing building. He presses his pen hard, broadening the line of his own building, making the image of the new structure contrast with the lighter of the old, a favourite technique in architectural drawings since the Renaissance. The emphasis in the extension is upon the upper grid, the long band of windows of the studio space. The lower section is blank, the solid stone of the walls.

The original building, a neo-Renaissance style art gallery built in 1917 by Cass Gilbert, is reduced to a series of arches indicating the entrance. Unity with the new is noted by the vertical pilasters and matching rooflines. A lone figure indicates scale.

Venturi, famous for his theory that architecture is but a decorated shed, here proves his point skilfully.

43

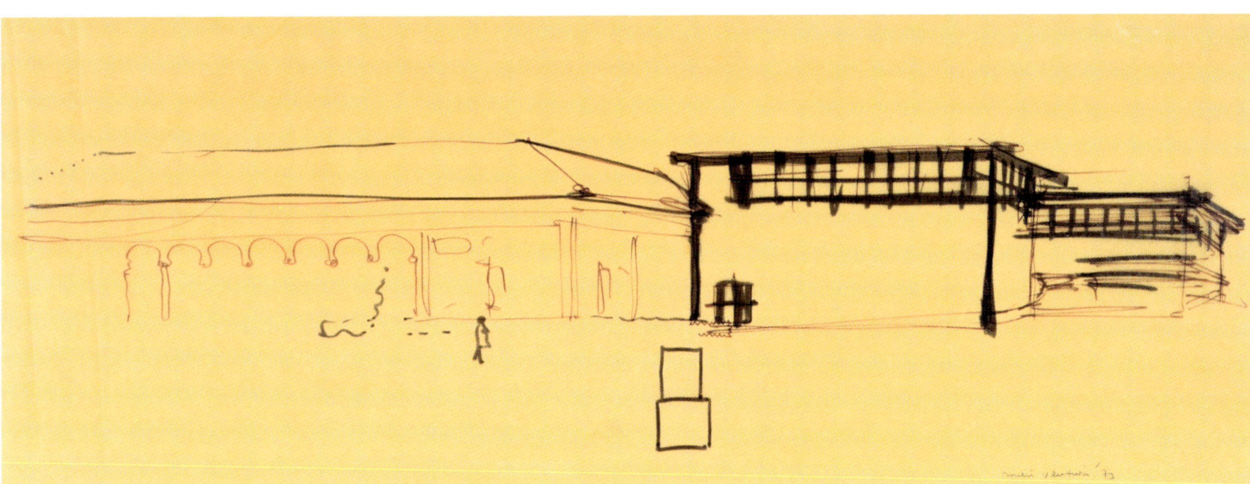

44 Oswald Mathias Ungers (born 1926)

Design for housing unit, Marburg, Germany, *c.*1976

Aerial perspective
Print with coloured washes on paper (290 x 290)
Lit.: Martin Kieren, *Oswald Mathias Ungers*. Zurich & London: Artemis, 1994, pp.90–93; O.M. Ungers, *Oswald Mathias Ungers: architektur 1951–1990*. Stuttgart: Deutsche Verlags-Anstalt, 1991, pp.82–99

44

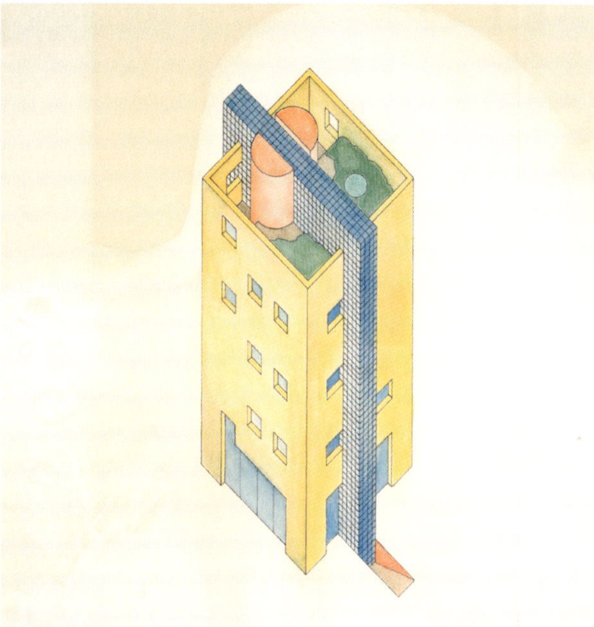

Although fifty years of age at the time of this design, Ungers was just about to break into architectural prominence . . . with this unbuilt project. He had been building since the early 1950s, but the designs Unger undertook at the invitation of the city of Marburg to develop a feasibility study for housing proved so successful that posters showing the many different types of housing units are still popularly available today.

For the project, Ungers designed house after house, each a variant in appearance – what Ungers called 'examples of morphological transformation' – but all colourful, three storeys high, similar in volume and with the same base measurements. These differing units could then be clustered together, suggesting the medieval houses of Marburg.

In this design example, the house is created out of cubic volumes and squares. These geometric forms have become the basis of Ungers's architecture, which he has employed to great success since this design in his many office buildings, libraries and institutions; the extension to the Hamburg Kunsthalle, built between 1986 and 1992, is a virtual excess of cubes and squares.

45 Michael Graves (born 1934)

Design for alterations & additions to the architect's own house, The Warehouse, Princeton, New Jersey, USA, 1976

Elevations
Inscribed: *Warehouse Solarium*
Dated: *1976*
Pencil & coloured pencil on tracing paper (approx. 290 x 445)
Lit.: Kenneth Powell, *Graves Residence: Michael Graves*. London: Phaidon, 1995; *Architects' drawings from the collection of Barbara Pine.* Evanston, Illinois: Mary and Leigh Block Gallery, Northwestern University, 1987, p.22 & reprd p.13

The Warehouse is Michael Graves's own home and very much created in the spirit of the architecture of Sir John Soane, whom Graves admires enormously, and especially Sir John Soane's Museum.

This delicate pencil drawing dates from 1976, just after Graves acquired a 1920s furniture depository building in Princeton, where he teaches at the university. It shows a section of his design for converting the hollow clay, brick and stucco structure into his new house. The form is dominated by the square and rectangle, most of it in glass to create a solarium. There is also a pediment, with a semi-ocular opening, an appropriate touch for Graves, who at the time of this drawing stood on threshold of becoming a leading architect of the Post-Modern movement.

In the early 1990s, Graves made extensive additions to The Warehouse, reinforcing Soane's influence in the use, for example, of internal shallow barrel vaults. Graves's fine collection of neo-classical furniture and objects makes the house very museum-like, and it is the architect's hope that his home may become an architectural study centre – again, paralleling Sir John Soane's Museum.

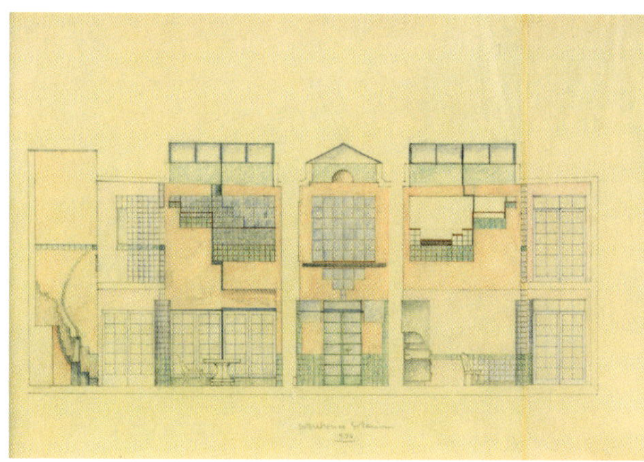 45

46 Michael Graves (born 1934)

Commemorative poster of the Portland Building, Portland, Oregon, USA, 1982

Inscribed: (in brown crayon, by architect) *The Portland Building / for Barbara* & (printed) *The Portland Building / Portland, Oregon / Dedication / October 2, 1982 / Michael Graves Architect / Francis J Ivancie Mayor*
Signed & dated: *Michael Graves / 1982*
Print with collage & mixed media (770 x 495)
Lit.: *Architects' drawings from the collection of Barbara Pine.* Evanston, Illinois: Mary and Leigh Block Gallery, Northwestern University, 1987, p.23; Karel Vogel Wheeler, Peter Arnell & Ted Bickford eds, *Michael Graves: buildings and projects 1966–1981*. London: Architectural Press, 1983

On this poster, from a limited edition of 150 created to commemorate the dedication of his Portland Building in Oregon, the architect Michael Graves has written a large dedication to his friend Barbara Pine.

With cheeky irony, Graves treats the image like a Cubist painting. A traditional perspective of the building is framed through a window with its curtain tied back, a favourite Cubist trick of looking through a café window. Here the contrast is between the massive power of the government building and the homeliness of the setting. Like an early Picasso or a George Braque, the work is made as a collage of wood and card, a montage of fractured segments, in this case representing parts of the Portland Building. For example, the curtain made of Japanese tissue paper mimics the shape of the swags on the side of the building; and, in turn, this is held in place by a tiny pair of light blue painted brackets imitating the giant corbels and keystone over the building entrance.

Even before it was finished, the Portland Building had become an icon of the new Post-Modernist style of which Michael Graves was a leader. With its over-scaled classical features, the building was painted in colours similar to this poster.

47 Aldo Rossi (1931–1997)

Design for an *armoire* (wardrobe), 1980

Sketch plans, elevations, perspectives & details
Inscribed: with some measurements
Signed & dated: *Aldo Rossi 80*
Pencil & coloured pencil on tracing paper (740 x 498)
Lit.: *Architects' drawings from the collection of Barbara Pine.* Evanston, Illinois: Mary and Leigh Block Gallery, Northwestern University, 1987, reprd p.34

46

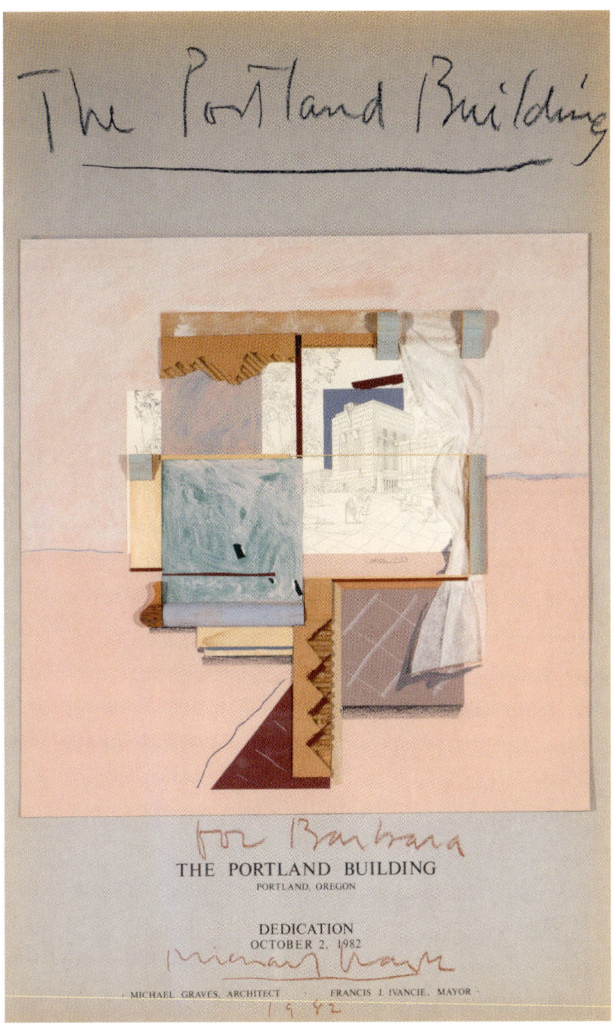

47

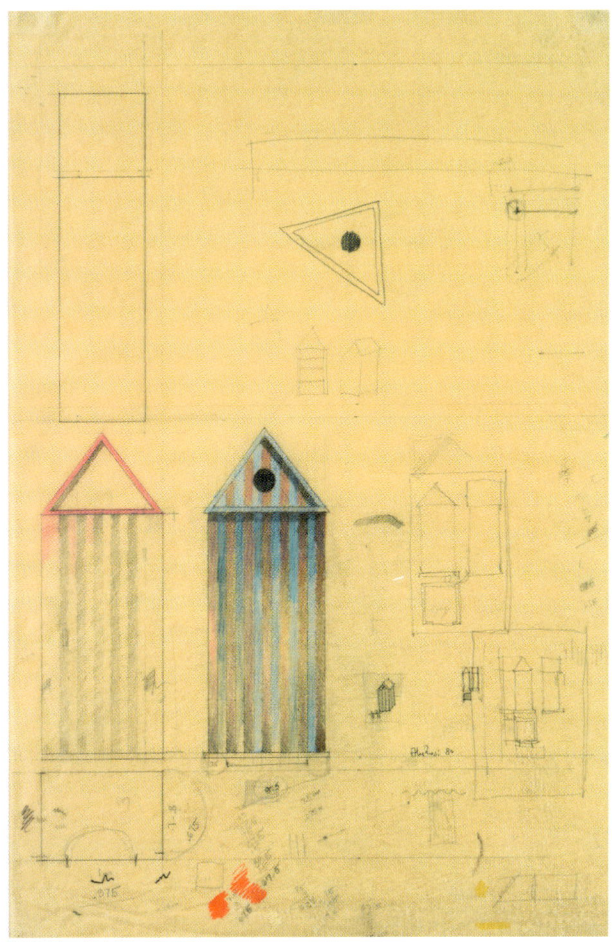

Aldo Rossi's design for an *armoire* is based upon the cabanas – seaside bathing huts which the architect encountered on the Italian island of Elba early in his career. These colourfully striped little structures were to figure prominently in Rossi's architectural and urban planning schemes, appearing in various forms in many of his projects. A most notable example was his unexecuted scheme for student housing in the mountain-side town of Chieti, in 1976, where enlarged versions of serried ranks of these striped cabanas, with doors and windows, lined the slopes.

Although the theme of the cabana as *armoire* appears to be light-hearted, in Rossi's hands it carries the overtones of classic architecture, noticeably with the pediment and oculus. Furthermore, the cabana occupied the architect's interest in monumental geometries, here emphasised by the bold and broad banding, as well as with colour, which came to play an important part in Rossi's later work. His last project, inaugurated the day after his death, was the Quartier Schützenstrasse in Berlin, a collection of buildings which presents a façade to the street of a wide variety of styles and colours – a late Post-Modern development.

A prototype of this *armoire* was made.

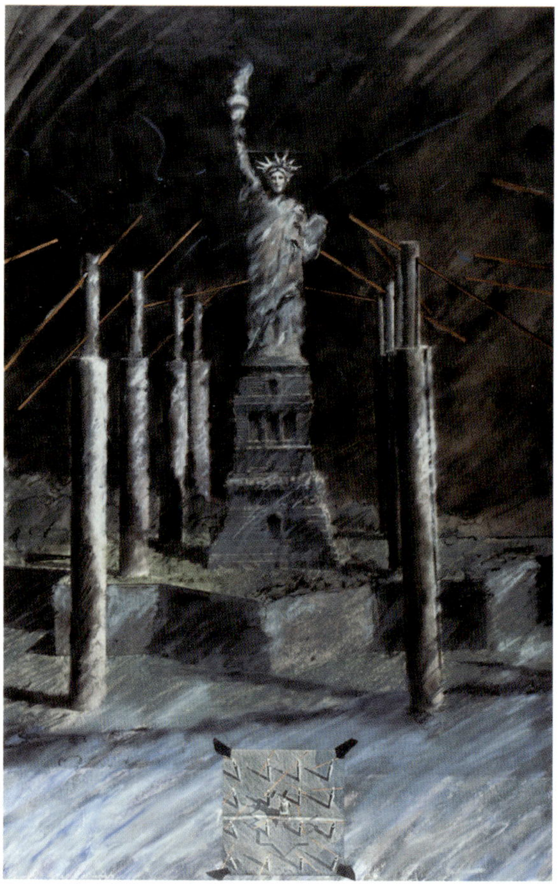

48

48 Billie Tsien (born 1949) & Tod Williams (born 1943)

Competition design for a Monument to the *Statue of Liberty*, 1980

Perspective with attached aerial perspective
Inscribed: As above
Signed: *Tod Williams Billie Tsien*
Coloured oil paints, crayon, gouache, gold paint, watercolour & black tape added with collage on paper (1090 x 700)
Lit.: *Architects' drawings from the collection of Barbara Pine.* Evanston, Illinois: Mary and Leigh Block Gallery, Northwestern University, 1987, reprd p.43

When the husband and wife partnership of Billie Tsien and Tod Williams entered this drawing in a competition in 1980, they had only just completed their first building. Today, these New York architects have gained a reputation for a series of cool, rational, beautifully detailed buildings, like the Phoenix Art Gallery and the American Folk Art Museum in New York.

The competition, sponsored by the American Institute of Architects, was based on the idea of celebrating the Statue of Liberty but without touching its sacred structure. In this dark and haunting perspective, Tsien and Williams have turned America's grandest lady into a symbol of Post-Modernism. The late nineteenth-century classicism of the Statue of Liberty sculpture and pedestal has been enclosed in a late twentieth-century temple, as if the statue of Athena has been restored to her altar within the ancient Parthenon. Cylindrical columns are crowned by rotating rods of copper, the material of the great figure herself, glowing in the night, attracting bolts of lighting, the fingers of God.

The bird's-eye view at the bottom, beautifully drawn like the rest of the drawing, shows the long sun-cast shadows from the columns; it has been attached to the drawing, deliberately carelessly, using bits of torn black tape.

49 Peter Shire (born 1947)

Design for an armchair, 1981

Side elevation & perspectives
Signed & dated: *Shire / 1981*
Pencil & watercolour (255 x 360)
Lit.: *Architects' drawings from the collection of Barbara Pine.* Evanston, Illinois: Mary and Leigh Block Gallery, Northwestern University, 1987, p.39, reprd p.37; Charlotte & Peter Fiell, *Design of the twentieth century*. Köln: Taschen, 1999, p.646

Here is a big, bold piece of Memphis furniture from a leader of this Anti-design group. Peter Shire had first made his name in creating bizarre teapots, attracting the attention of the Italian architect and designer Ettore Sottsass, who asked him to join his Memphis Group in 1981, the year of its foundation . . . and the year of this design.

Although this chair does not seem to have gone into production, a prototype was made. Like Shire's other Memphis furniture, such as the Brazil console table and particularly the related Bel Air armchair – for which this drawing may be a preliminary design – the object playfully distorts any notion of good taste and is composed of outsized parts and a riot of bright colours.

Shire thrives on the clashing kaleidoscope of colours and forms he finds in Mexico and his native Los Angeles. His own house is a Post-Modern shock of juxtaposed colours and materials, with painted lime vintage chairs mixed with such pieces as his own hot pink armchair, another design variation on the chair in this drawing.

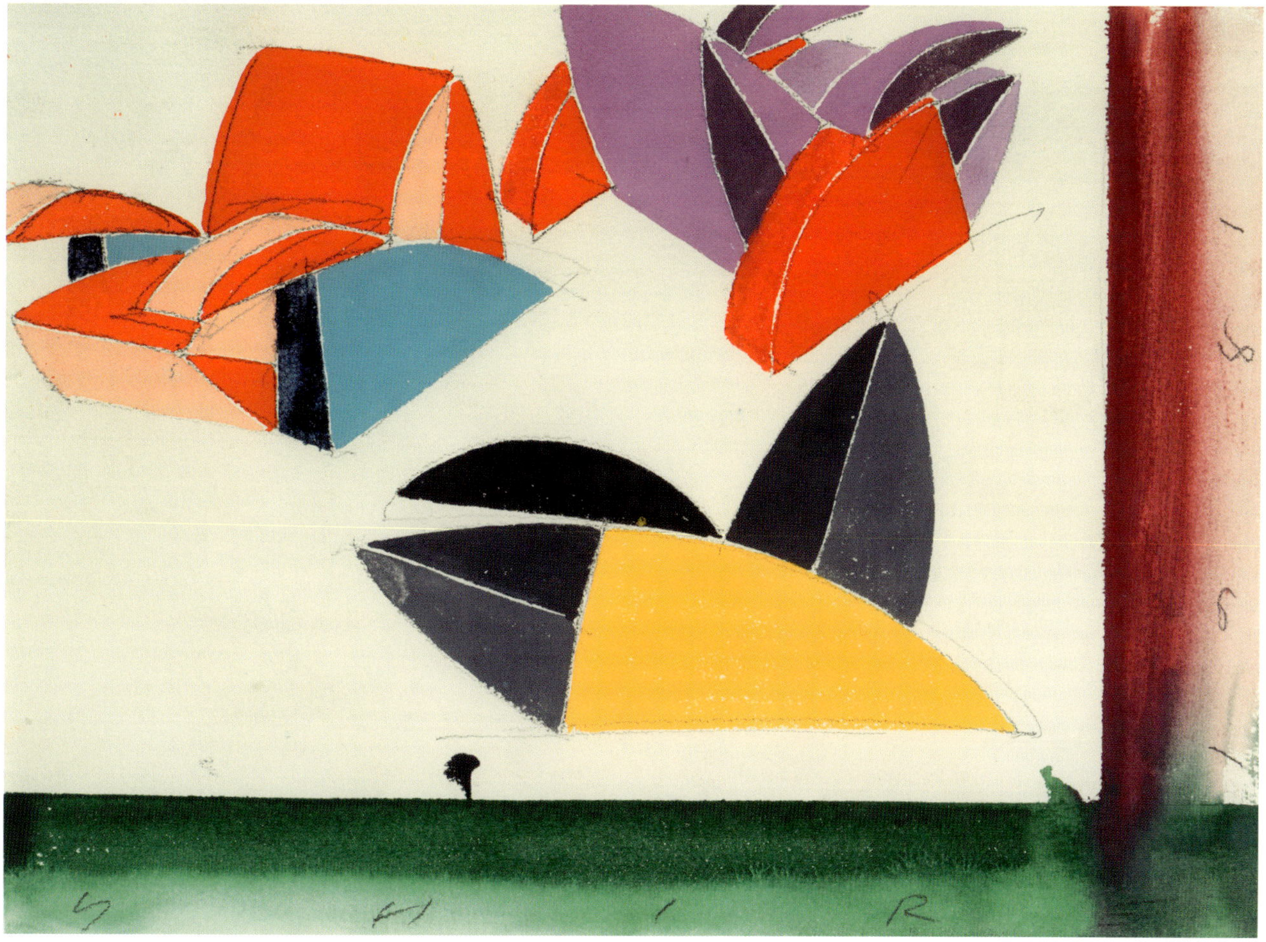 49

50 Frank O. Gehry (born 1929)

Studies (2) for a tract house, 1982

Sketch perspectives
Inscribed: (No.1) *Walls & Objects* (No.2) *Objects & Painted Walls*
Signed & dated: (each) *F Gehry '82*
(each) Brown pen & coloured crayon on paper (130 x 210)
Lit.: Francesco Dal Co and Kurt W. Forster, *Frank O. Gehry: the complete works*. New York: Monacelli, 1998, p.232; *Architects' drawings from the collection of Barbara Pine.* Evanston, Illinois: Mary and Leigh Block Gallery, Northwestern University, 1987, one study reprd p.21; Mildred Friedman ed., *Gehry talks: architecture + process*. New York: Rizzoli, 1999, p.72

This pair of drawings, from 1982, are design studies for a tract, or extended, house. Gehry had been invited to submit designs for an exhibition about tract housing at the Leo Castelli gallery in Los Angeles. His solution was a group of pavilions, each containing a specific function of the house; in other words, one was the living room, another a bedroom, and so on. Shape, texture, colour: each played its part in this 'collection of objects in a landscape', as Gehry referred to such village assemblies.

Although the exhibition never took place, these studies had a profound influence upon Gehry's architecture at this period in the 1980s. A striking example was the Schnabel House in Brentwood, California, designed and built between 1986 and 1989. Marna Schnabel was an architect in Gehry's office, and had constructed the unexhibited cardboard model of the tract house (cardboard was a favoured material of Gehry's at the time, as attested by the cardboard furniture designs in the Barbara Pine collection). So much had Schnabel liked Gehry's tract house that she and her husband commissioned Gehry to build something similar. The Schnabel house, a very large residence, is thus a series of pavilions, each reflecting the clients' specific requirements.

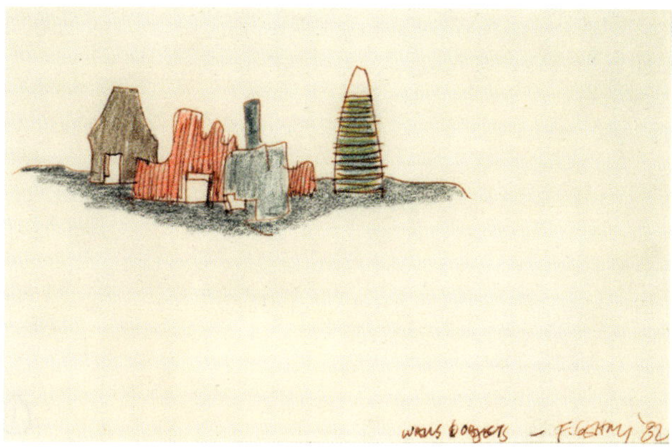 50

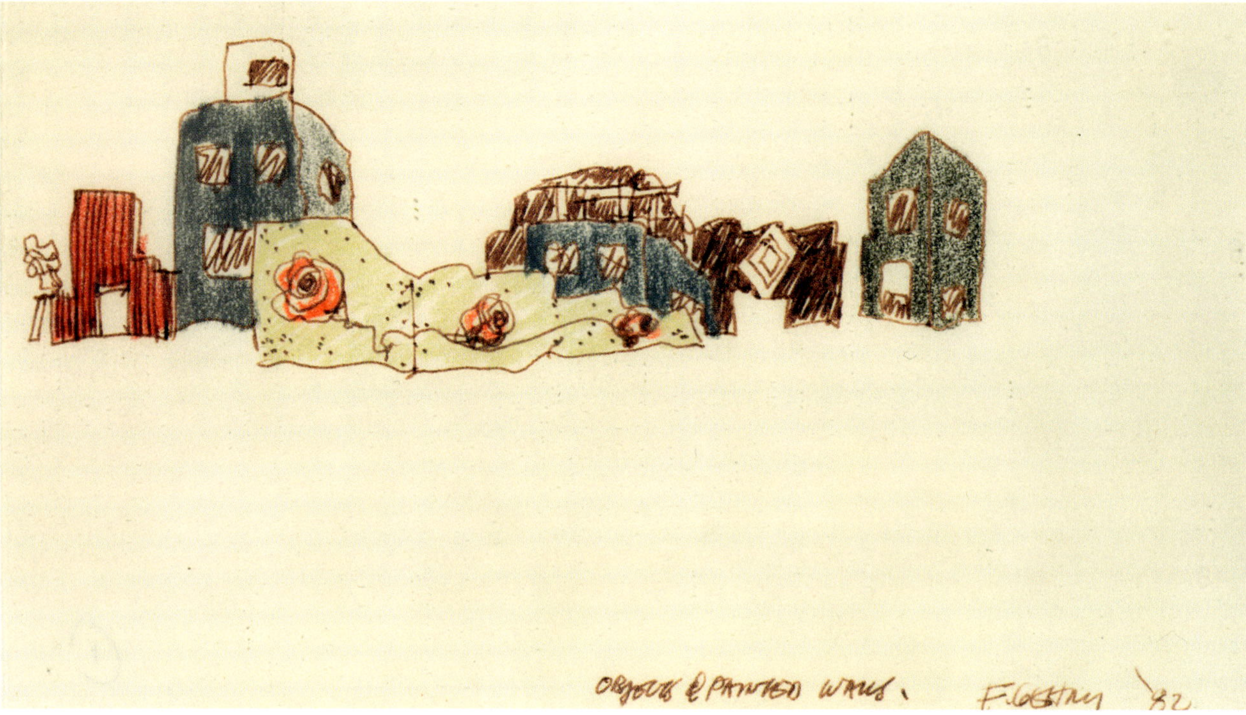

50

51 Frank O. Gehry (born 1929)

Sketch designs for a cardboard chair, 1982

Signed & dated: *F. Gehry '82*
Red & blue pencil on yellow ruled paper (approx. 240 x 185)
Lit.: J. Fiona Rahgeb ed., *Frank Gehry, architect*. New York: Guggenheim Museum Publications, 2001, pp.24–27, 56–59

The architect Frank Gehry began designing furniture made of cardboard early in his career. Intrigued by the tough resilience of cardboard, Gehry began experimenting with layering, stacking, glueing and cutting multiple sheets in a variety of forms. The malleability of the material allowed Gehry to create some astonishing furniture shapes. Some of his first pieces, from his Easy Edges series, were commercially produced in 1972, in seventeen types: tables and chairs, even a bar and bar stools. The most well-known is the Squiggle Chair.

Between 1979 and 1982, Gehry returned to designing cardboard furniture, but this time concentrating more upon the use of less dense and thicker cardboard, often corrugated. This drawing comes from this second series, known as Experimental Edges.

The two chair designs in this drawing are variants: the thin L-shape frame for the base and back has a solid look, probably intended to be made of hardboard. But the wide seat and back would be of cardboard. Interestingly, these sections do not meet, leaving a void at the corner, making way for the wavy ends of the seat and back to give a comfortable springiness when sat upon. The abstract pattern in the lower right is a plan for how the pieces can be cut from a large sheet of cardboard.

Although this chair did not go into production, several corrugated pieces from this series have become design classics, like the wide-bodied Little Beaver chair and ottoman.

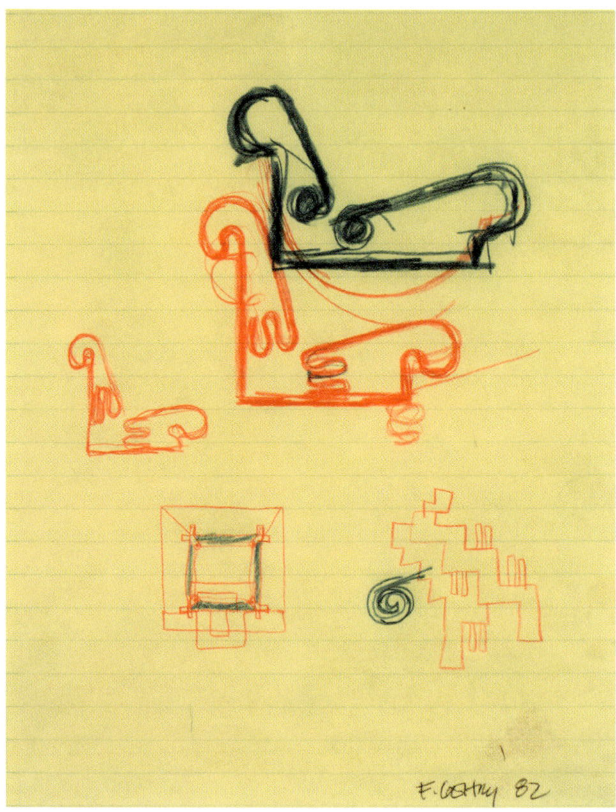

51

52 Frank O. Gehry (born 1929)

Studies (2) for fish table lamps and snake lamps, 1984

Sketch elevations & perspectives
Signed & dated: (each) *F Gehry '84*
(each) Brown pen on sketch book pages (275 x 352)
Lit.: J. Fiona Raghel ed., *Frank Gehry, Architect*. New York: Guggenheim Museum, 2001, pp.80–83; *Architects' drawings from the collection of Barbara Pine*. Evanston, Illinois: Mary and Leigh Block Gallery, Northwestern University, 1987, one study reprd p.20

Frank Gehry was one of the designers invited by the Formica Company to present their new laminate product, Colorcore. The architect's approach was highly unorthodox: instead of the usual use of laminate as a veneer for fixtures and furniture, Gehry turned the material into furniture . . . into lamp sculptures.

Admiring Colorcore's translucent qualities, and then accidentally shattering a sheet of the laminate into little pieces, Gehry realized that he could turn the material into one of his favourite shapes, the fish, and also into snakes because of the scaly nature of the broken shards. The fish has been a repeating and playful motif in Gehry's repertoire, used for example in his Fishdance Restaurant in Kobe, Japan, with its bar in the form of a coiled snake, as well as a giant fish mesh sculpture at the Barcelona Vila Olimpica.

These design drawings show the fish lamps placed on sharded beds and pedestals while the snake lamps are made to curl around objects. About three dozen of these unique pieces were made by New City Editions.

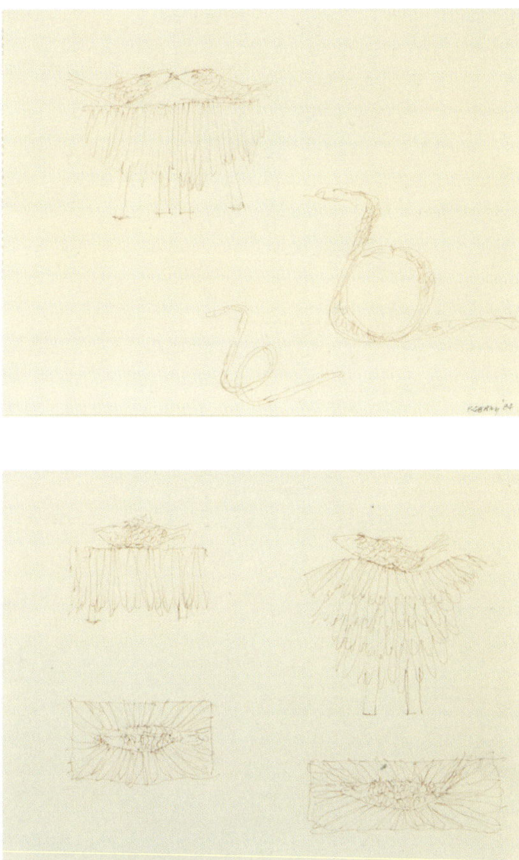

52

53 Helmut Jahn (born 1940)

Sketch designs for South Ferry Plaza, New York, 1985

Plans & elevations
Inscribed: FT /A: *Eiffel-T / B2: B1 Gate / C3 Boat / Light-House / C1 / C2*
Signed & dated: *Helmut Jahn 4.18.85*
Brown & blue pen on office paper printed *Muphy/Jahn* (215 x 215)
Lit.: *Architects' drawings from the collection of Barbara Pine*. Evanston, Illinois: Mary and Leigh Block Gallery, Northwestern University, 1987, reprd p.26

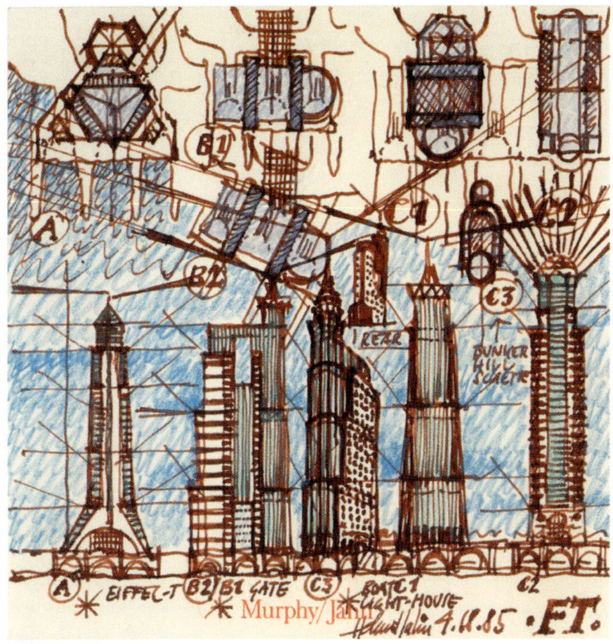

53

Helmut Jahn loves to draw skyscrapers . . . and build them. He can fill sheet upon sheet with his neat and precisely drawn designs, landscaping the page as if writing a hieroglyphic text, from left to right in horizontal rows. This is a typical example. Here the architect experiments with five ideas for a scheme which never got off the ground – a new terminal for the Staten Island Ferry, which would have been dramatically located at the southern tip of Manhattan. Integrated with the waterside terminal was also to be a fifty-storey high-rise office and hotel complex. Over the triple arches of the terminal is a raised podium – the plaza – affording views across the water (evoked by the wavy blue lines) to such landmarks as the Statue of Liberty.

Above each of the five elevations in this drawing is the correlating plan and sometimes even a variant. Jahn gives each proposal a title, at times simply a letter and number. But frequently he assigns a name which relates to the tower shape. The first, for example, is *Eiffel*, for obvious reasons. There is also *Light-House*; and *Bunker Hill*, in response to the great granite obelisk monument on the site of the first battle of the American Civil War, near Boston. At the time of this drawing, Jahn was working in the Post-Modern style of the 1970s and '80s, using historical references. For example, his design for the Messetrum skyscraper built in Frankfurt, Germany, and begun the same year as this drawing, is a modern sleek tower crowned by a glass pyramid.

54 Mario Botta (born 1943)

Design for the Quinta chair, for Alias, *c.*1985

Sketch side elevation, perspectives & details
Inscribed: *Vx* [ie. 5th] *Alias*
Signed: *Mario Botta*
Black crayon on paper (310 x 490)

Quinta means fifth, and this was the fifth piece of furniture which the Swiss architect Mario Botto designed for the Italian furniture company Alias. It went into production at the same time as Botto's Sesta armchair.

This assured drawing, like the chair itself, sums up Botta's overriding concern, expressed in his many theoretical writings, asserting that design is as an abstraction and that it must relate to man. Seated on the chair in this drawing, in the large perspective on the left and in the side elevation, is a ghostly figure which almost merges with the object. The two are one.

Botto said of this chair design that it was inspired by an encounter he had when a young man in Paris, in 1965, when he visited the Swiss sculptors, brothers Alberto and Diego Giacometti. Seated at their table, Botto was impressed by Alberto's designs for the chairs which looked somewhat like people and thus gave the impression that even when there were no diners, the table looked in use.

The Quinta is all metal, made of a slender tube frame, with two perforated bent metal sheets for back and seat.

55 Steven Holl (born 1947)

Design for housing, Porta Vittoria, Milan, Italy, 1986

Sketch plan, perspective & details
Signed & dated: *S. Holl '86*
Pencil & coloured washes on paper (238 x 336)
Lit.: *Anchoring: Steven Holl: selected projects 1975-1991*. 3rd edition. Princeton, New Jersey: Princeton University Press, 1991, pp.96–107

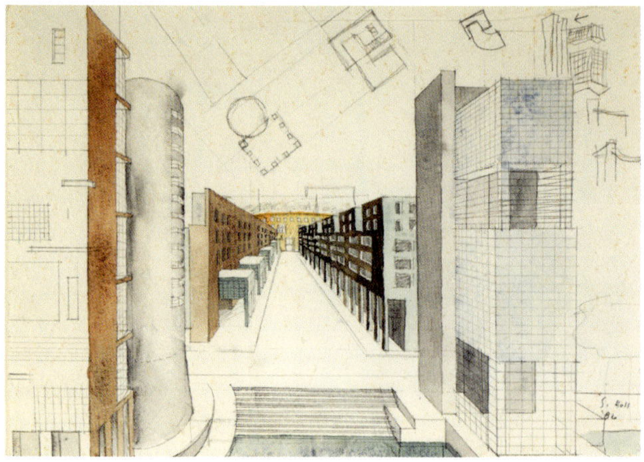
55

The American architect Steven Holl, known for his sensitive handling of urban landscape, was invited in 1986 to take part in the XVII Triennale of Milan by undertaking a suggested theoretical redevelopment of a section of the host city. The Porta Vittoria is a heavily industrialised area with a disused rail freight yard. Holl's scheme sought a mixed redevelopment: housing, offices, hotels, and transportation hubs like a bus station and air terminal station.

This drawing is for an avenue of housing, different on both sides of the street, terminating in the curving yellow form of a civic building which Holl described as the 'bureaucratic double-flux slab'. The vista is flanked in the foreground by a gate, a *porta*: the building on the left with its semi-rounded tower recalls the Porta Vittoria's medieval fortifications, and the building on the right is a contrasting geometrical glass façade. These structures guard the steps to a water basin.

This scheme served as a prelude to Holl's large housing development in the new Japanese town of Makuhari where the architect employed similar ideas in design and concept, especially the contrasting appearance within unit groups.

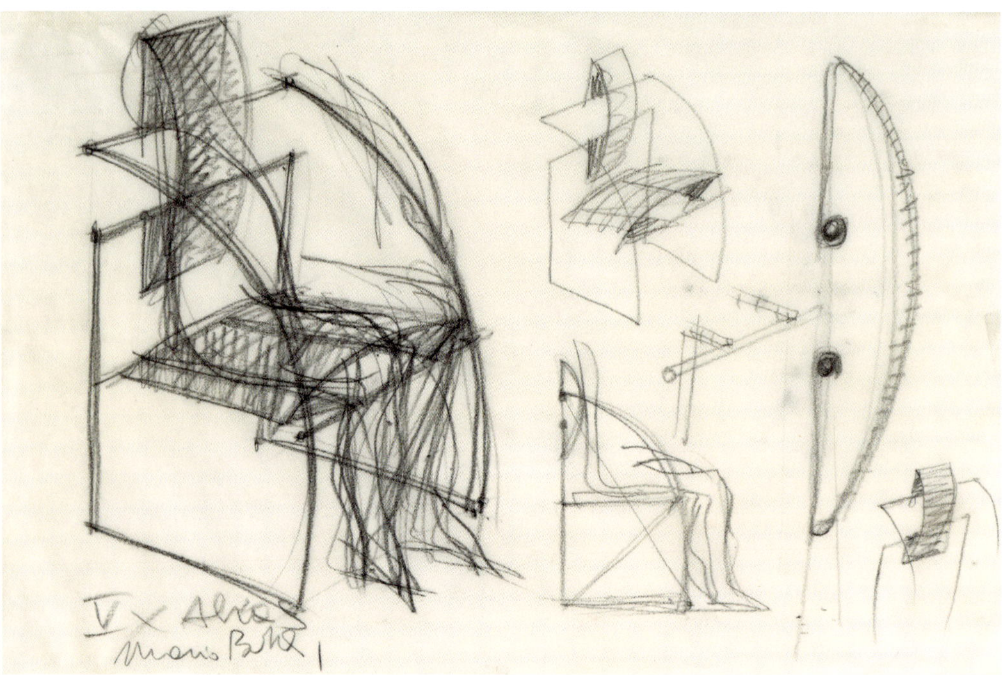
54

56 Peter Eisenman (born 1932)

Sketches & text, 1990

Inscribed: As below & *Pedro Feduchi / Antonio Ortiz / ABCynthia / deconstructio / arch / here and / now / Arch should take place / only way to do it / Central core vs / marginal. / The architectural / reality / applied art / Architecture will always look like arch. / Principles & tunes / Arch Principles underlie. / Automatic. / Automaticism of context / Traces and imprints*
Dated: *11 Julio 90 Escorial*
Blue & red pen on letterhead paper for *Universidad / Complutense / Cursos de Verano* (295 x 205)

The American architect Peter Eisenman is as strong a theoretician as he is a practitioner. He made this sheet of sketches and text while visiting the summer school in the Spanish town of El Escorial in 1990. He has noted the names of the two Spanish companions he is no doubt conversing with while he jots down and illustrates his points: the architect and writer Pedro Feduchi and the important Seville architect Antonio Ortiz.

In three-dimensional lettering, Eisenman writes 'ABCynthia', a play on his wife's name, Cynthia Davidson, who is a partner in his architectural practice. Underneath appears 'deconstructio', Spanish for 'deconstruction', the movement of which Eisenman is a prime exponent. The exploding diagrams across this sheet are perfect examples of some of Eisenman's ideas on the de-construction of his designs, which he explores in such areas as distorting, twisting, morphing, warping, slippage, blurring, etc.

These diagrams principally seem to touch upon two such concerns of Eisenman's at the period he created this sheet: folding and bars. The unfolding L-shapes, drawn in plan and perspective as if in motion, would seem to relate to an unbuilt project from two years previously, the Casa Guardiola, a house which had an entrance squeezed between a façade configured like this pair of expanding Ls. The long bars of the other diagrams again illustrate form in motion, and relate to two projects the architect was working on: the unbuilt Olympic Hotel in Banyoles near Barcelona, and the Greater Columbus Convention Center in Ohio, completed in 1993, which has a similar finger-like structure.

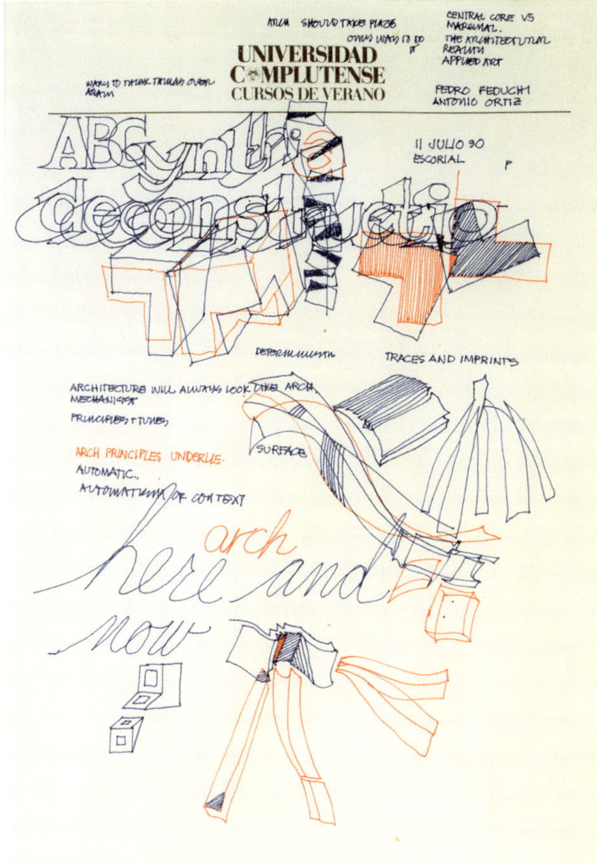

56

57 Ben van Berkel (born 1957)

Design for the eastern entrance & service building for the Piet Hein Tunnel, Amsterdam, Netherlands, *c.*1990

Plan & elevation
Signed: *B*
Pencil, pen, coloured inks & orange & red crayon on paper (approx. 300 x 400)
Lit.: Ben van Berkel & Caroline Box, *UN Studio un fold*. Rotterdam: NAI, 2002, pp.22–25, reprd p.24; Ben van Berkel & Caroline Bos, *Move*. Amsterdam: UN Studio & Goose Press, 1999, vol. 1, pp.160–73

Ben van Berkel and his wife Caroline Box are the leading partners in UN Studio, a very hot architectural practice based in Amsterdam. One of their best-known works is the Erasmus Bridge in Rotterdam, completed in 1996, which in its elegant sweep shows the influence of the Spanish architect-engineer Santiago Calatrava, for whom van Berkel worked in the late 1980s.

In the mid-1980s, van Berkel had studied at the Architectural Association, London, under the architect Zaha Hadid, and the inspiration of her highly individual drawing style is evident in this van Berkel drawing. It shows the entrance and service building to the Piet Hein Tunnel, a tunnel created to link the new and very fashionable building developments growing up in Amsterdam's old Eastern docks. Van Berkel's drawing style, alternating precision with abandon, captures both the purity of the architecture and the rough topography of the project. In the top elevation, the fixed black lines of the layered building and long tunnel entrance are overlaid with the streaks of red and yellow coloured crayon indicating the speed of traffic as it flashes by; while in the plan below the smeared blue ink depicts the icy cold waters of the River Ij lapping the sides of the tunnel.

58 Daniel Libeskind (born 1946)

Three sheets of sketches for the Jewish Museum, Berlin, Germany, *c.*1990

(1) Three sketch perspectives, bottom one labelled *Galleries*
Signed: (letterhead) *Daniel Libeskind / Bregenzer Strasse 3, 1000 Berlin 15, West Germany. Tel 030-8831023/24. Fax 8831216*
Inscribed: As above
Brown pen on letterhead paper (295 x 208)
(2) Sketch schematic plan
Inscribed: *Jewish Museum*
Brown pen on 4-ring binder paper (115 x 80)
(3) Sketch schematic plan
Inscribed: (parts labelled) *Absolute Future, Absolute Past, Elsewhere (not future / not past)*
Brown & black pen on sketchbook page (115 x 80)

57

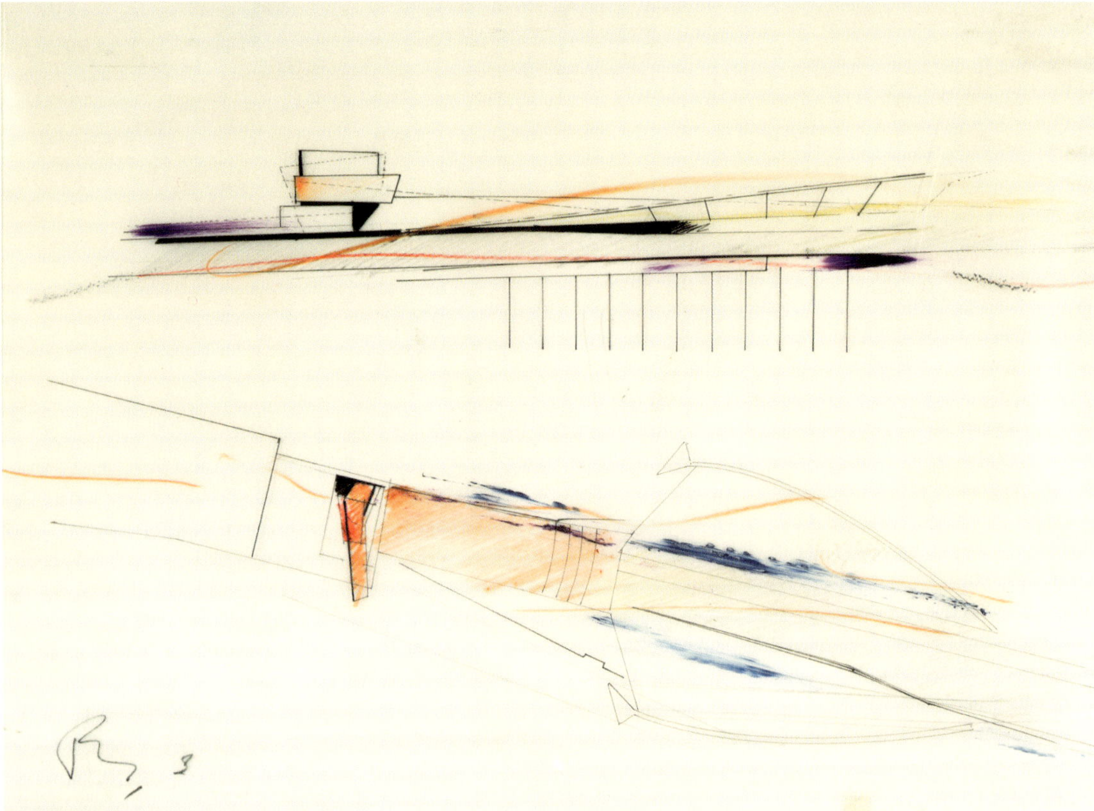

58

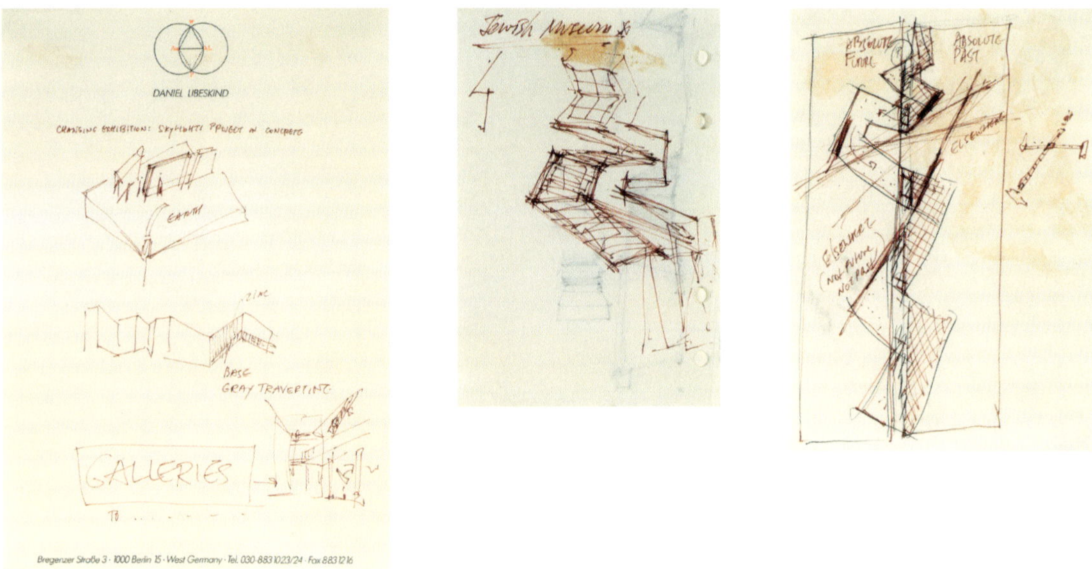

The Jewish Museum is one of the most powerful architectural works created in the late twentieth century. Although presenting Jewish history in Berlin and Germany, the museum has come to symbolize the Holocaust. Even before completion in 2001, when the building was open to the public for eighteen months, visitors were overwhelmed by the disturbing effects of Daniel Libeskind's deconstructivist architecture with its spiralling walls, sloping floors and windows that were slashed like wounds.

In the smaller two of this trio of drawings, Libeskind has sketched variant plans for the museum; the sketch within the boxed line is the form the building took when completed. Interpreted as a broken Star of David, the zigzag configuration is a path leading the visitor through galleries representing various encounters in Jewish history, which Libeskind has abstracted with ideas such as 'absolute future' and 'absolute past' in the larger drawing. As built, the architect placed a 'void' running through this lightening bolt configuration, an empty raw space, symbolic of that which is absent, vanished, but still present.

59 Ron Arad (born 1951)

Studies for furniture for an exhibition, *c.*1993

Inscribed: *C.B.C. / in / box / 2RNot / Bronze / Happy Days*
Pencil & red & blue crayon on tracing paper (208 x 296)

This is a drawing of furniture designs made by Ron Arad in preparation for an exhibition on the theme of boxes, held in Milan at the Krizia Space in 1994. On this small sheet, Arad has tightly packed almost two dozen sketches of different chairs and, in the lower right, complete with a potted plant, a perspective seen from below of a bookshelf unit.

Trained as an architect, Ron Arad came to prominence in the early 1980s with the extraordinary furniture and objects he sold at his Covent Garden studio in London, One-Off. Many of his chairs are late twentieth-century furniture classics, including the Rover chair, made from a Rover car seat placed within a tubular metal structure, and the Well Tempered chair, a bulbous piece of bolted steel.

All the chairs sketched here are created from metal and are mainly works which Arad had created in recent years. Several are labelled including the *C.B.C.*, signifying 'chair by its cover' (1989–90) and the *2 R Not* (1992). The designer plays with variations, suggesting that the 2 R Not be made in bronze, differing from the usual black steel, so that it can be turned on four of its sides to create different seating configurations. Arad also considers putting it into a box. At this period, Arad often investigated boxing his furniture, usually in two sections of metal, so that the box itself could be used as chairs after unpacking, and thus even further multiply the seating options.

60 Michael Maltzen (born 1959)

Preliminary design for signage, Museum of Modern Art, Queens (MoMA QNS), New York, USA, *c.*2001

Three perspectives
Pen on paper (300 x 226)

In May 2002, the Museum of Modern Art (MoMA) on West 53rd Street in New York temporarily closed and underwent extensive rebuilding to designs by Yoshio Taniguchi, grandly reopening in October 2004. As a temporary venue, MoMA decamped to Long Island City, Queens, converting a former stapler factory for exhibitions, a library, study centre and storage, some of which facilities have remained.

The architect for MoMA QNS was the Los Angeles based Michael Maltzen. In this drawing, Maltzen explores how to make the signage on top of the building an eye-catching feature. As the principal approach to the temporary museum was from an elevated section of Line 7 of the New York subway, in these three views the architect sketches out the sequence as the train moves towards and past the big MoMA letters.

This tactic proved unsatisfactory, because the acronym is read in reverse on approach. However, Maltzen's final solution as erected was a brilliant deconstructive installation: the sign was fractured, the lettering split up, until a sudden moment just before the train entered the station, when they all came together to spell MoMA.

Illustrated overleaf

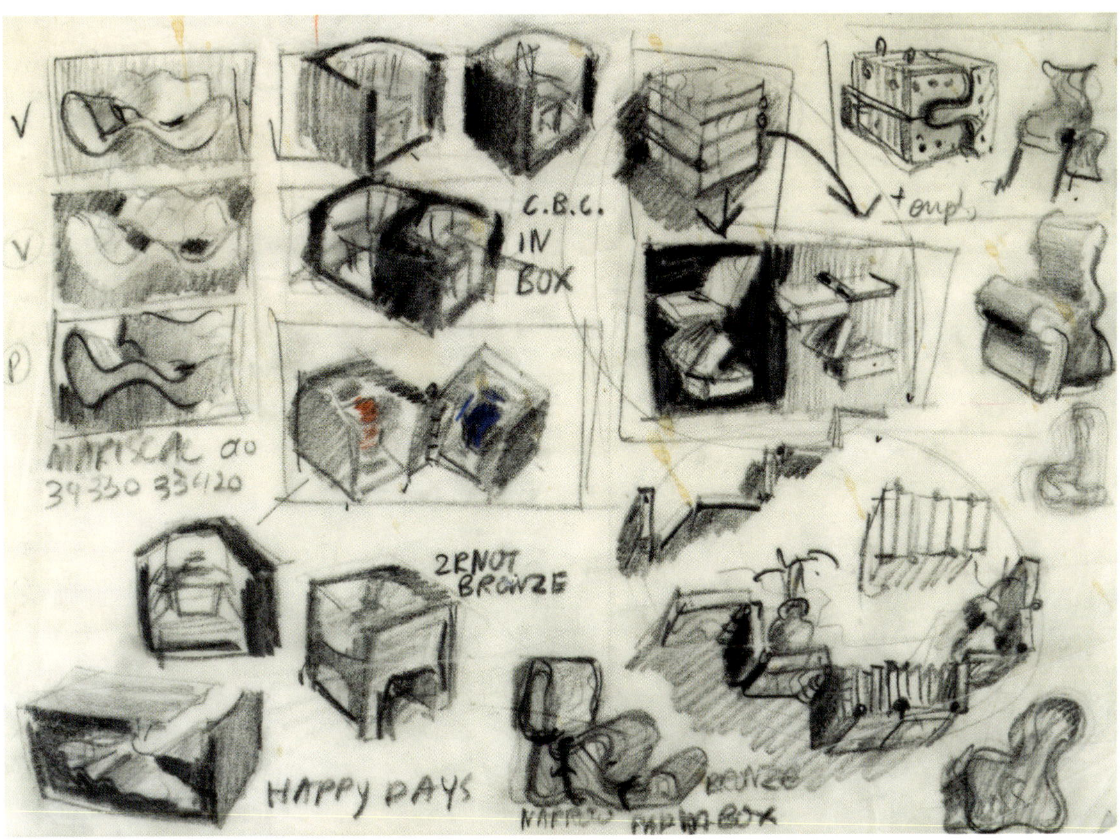

59

NEIL BINGHAM BIOGRAPHY

Neil Bingham, BA (Hons), Ph.D, is an independent scholar and writer on architecture, design and contemporary culture. From 1986 to 2003 he was the Assistant Curator at the Drawings Collection, Royal Institute of British Architects. His most recent publications include *Fantasy Architecture 1500–2036*. London: Hayward Gallery, 2004; *Modern Retro: Living with Mid-Century Style*. London & New York: Ryland, Peters & Small, 3rd edition, 2005; and *The New Boutique: Fashion and Design*. London & New York: Merrell, 2005.

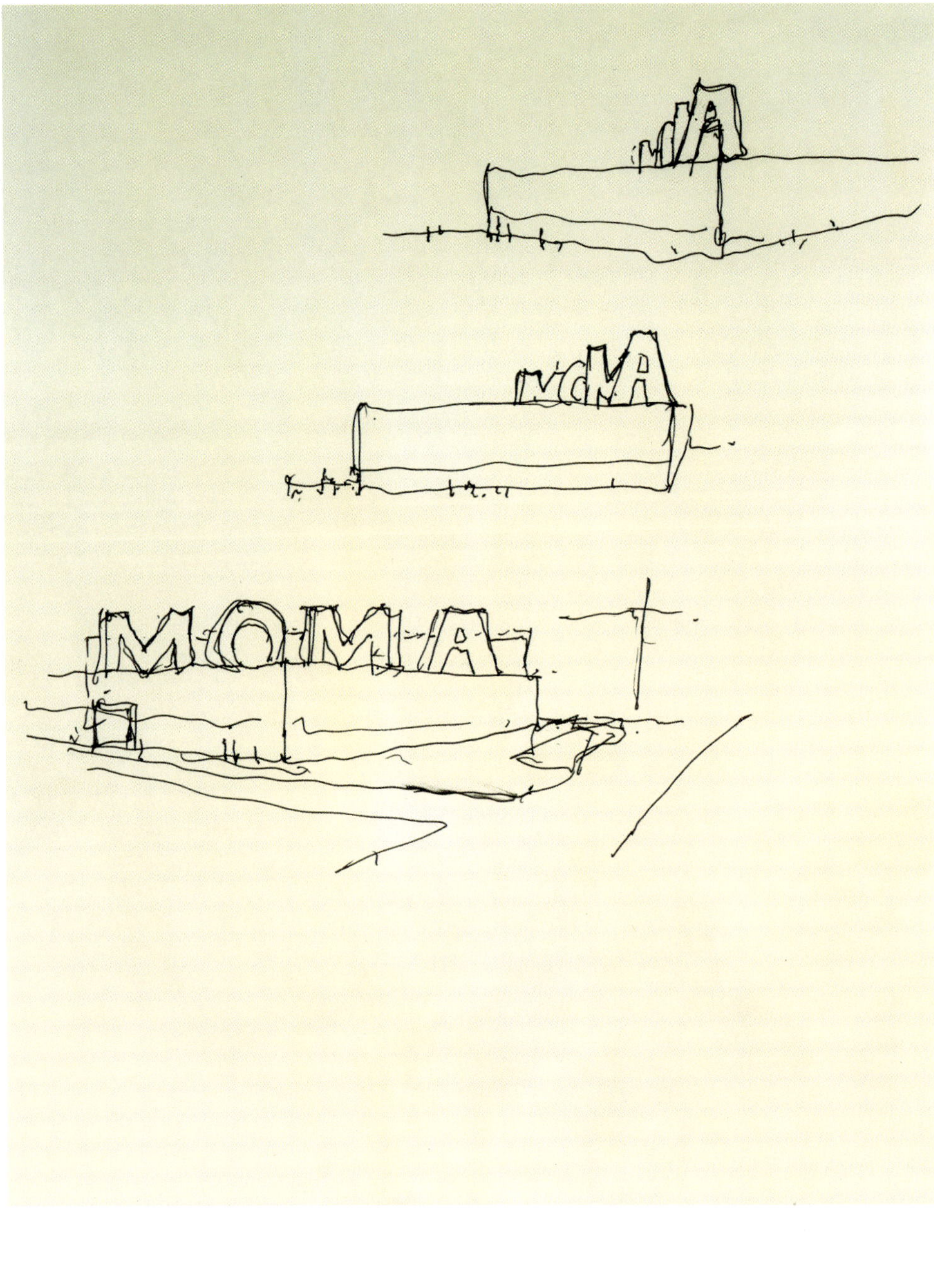

60